The Tribulation Survival Ma
Millions Have Disappeared off the
and You are Left Behind –

CW00498018

By

Paul McCarty

NOTE: This book is **NOT copyrighted** and is for the sole purpose of helping the tribulation saints, those left on the earth and saved after the rapture (these are redeemed during the Seven Year Tribulation Period - Daniel's 70th Week). The goal is to help these tribulation saints to understand the tragic events that are about to come upon the entire earth. All or part of this work can be reproduced and distributed without permission from the author. Any of the 144,000 chosen Jewish Witnesses (Revelation chapter 7 and Revelation chapter 14) and those that serve with them are encouraged to correct any and all mistakes in this book and retranslate/redistribute as they see best to the tribulation saints around the world!

This series of books is dedicated to all of **the tribulation saints** – more will be ask of you than of any other Christians throughout the course of human history!

All scripture quotations are from the Authorized (King James) Version. Where portions of a verse are in **bold,** underlined, colored, or set forth in CAPITAL LETTERS, it is for the purpose of the author's emphasis and does not represent a revision of the text.

Throughout this book I have *Real Time Updates* so you understand what was going on in my area of the world when I wrote that portion of the book. These *Real Time Updates* always begin with the time and date and are in *blue italicized font.*

1st Edition – Published October 2019

Table of Contents

Chapter 1: INTRODUCTION – PLEASE GET BORN AGAIN NOW – IT IS NOT TOO LATE!

*Real Time Update: 0200 Hours; November 1, 2016: I have finally decided to begin this book this morning. The rapture (catching up) of all truly born again believers (redeemed saints) has not happened yet at the time of this writing – although I expect it very soon. The scriptures are clear (**Matthew 24:36-51**) that no man knows the day nor the hour, but I believe the season for the first phase of the LORD's second coming, referred to as the rapture by many believers, is upon us and very near. I was born in 1965 and currently live in Alabama in the United States of America. I was born again as a 22 year old young man in August of 1988, just before my senior year in college.*

*If this world wide cataclysmic event involving the sudden disappearance of millions of the earth's population has already taken place, you will not be able to find me on this earth anymore. For I am one of those saints who has disappeared. I have been resurrected (**Genesis 5:21-24; Hebrews 11:5**) and I am now in heaven with the LORD Jesus Christ. I will return with Him at the Revelation (the second phase of His second coming) in exactly Seven Years (360 days = a year) from the signing of the peace treaty with the Antichrist and many others, including the Nation of Israel (Daniel's 70th week). At this time the LORD will destroy all of the followers of the Antichrist at the battle of Armageddon and set up His 1000 year Kingdom on the Earth. I know I will be returning with Him in my glorified resurrected body according to **Zachariah 14:5; Jude vs 14-15; Revelation 5:9-10; and Revelation 19:11-21**.*

We have a Presidential Election here in the United States one week from today. I believe that even though Donald Trump is behind in almost all the polls; that he will win the Presidency and be the next President of the United States. I will explain my reason for this belief later in this book when I discuss the role of the United States during the tribulation period.

Throughout this book I will have these ***Real Time Updates*** as detailed above so you know that I wrote these words before the rapture (disappearance) of the church age saints. I will always begin these real time updates with the time and date in *blue italics*.

The purpose of this book is to help you navigate through the most difficult time in human history on the face of the earth – commonly called the **Tribulation Period**. There is no copyright on this book as I want to get it into the hands of as many of those left behind on the earth as possible. If you are left behind please copy or send the digital version to as many people as possible so they have a chance of getting born again and surviving the tribulation period to see the glorious appearing of the Messiah (the LORD Jesus Christ). Many of you will not survive the tribulation period, but will be murdered (executed) for your faith in the LORD Jesus Christ. Please trust Him in this matter and realize you will obtain a better resurrection as His martyr. You will also rule and reign with Him in your glorified (resurrected) body in His literal 1000 year kingdom on the earth (**Revelation 20:4**).

My Quick Estimate of the Number of People that Vanished in the Rapture: I thought I would begin this book by taking a stab at the number of people that vanished from the earth. Only the LORD truly knows those that are His. No matter how many people claim to be Christians, only those that are truly born again and have the Holy Spirit of God living inside of them will have disappeared in the rapture to be with Jesus forever. I believe infants (including those in the womb) and young children who have not yet partaken of the tree of the knowledge of good and evil (who have not reached the age of reason where they know right from wrong) will also have disappeared at the rapture. Many countries who have very few Christians and very little gospel influence will still be greatly affected by the rapture because of all the infants and young children that vanished when Jesus came in the air to receive (rapture) His saints. Please do not worry or fret if you lost a young child or a child in the womb. I promise you they are safe in heaven with the LORD Jesus Christ, and you will see them again if you get born again yourself during this Seven Year Tribulation Period.

Please read this entire series of books and do not believe the lies from the politicians, the news media, and Satan himself as they attempt to explain away the sudden disappearance of millions of people. See the verses that follow which explain that (with the exception of the infants and young children that vanished) all of those that were raptured were born again believers with the Holy Spirit of God living inside of them. Those of you left behind were not true born again believers at the time of the rapture. You may have been religious, but you were not saved or you would have also been taken with the other believers. Maybe you were trusting your good works to get you to heaven and not the shed blood of the LORD Jesus Christ alone (**Colossians 1:14**), plus nothing, minus nothing. See the verses that follow:

Ephesians 2:8-9 – "⁸ For **by grace are ye saved through faith**; and that not of yourselves: *it is* the gift of God: ⁹ **not of works**, lest any man should boast."

1ˢᵗ John 5:11-13 –"¹¹And this is the record, that God hath given to us eternal life, and this life is in his Son. **¹²He that hath the Son hath life;** *and* **he that hath not the Son of God hath not life.**¹³ These things have I written unto you that believe on the name of the Son of God; that ye may know that ye have eternal life, and that ye may believe on the name of the Son of God."

John 7:37-39 – "³⁷ In the last day, that great *day* of the feast, Jesus stood and cried, saying, If any man thirst, let him come unto me, and drink. ³⁸ He that believeth on me, as the scripture hath said, out of his belly shall flow rivers of living water. ³⁹ (But this spake he of **the Spirit, which they that believe on him should receive**: for the Holy Ghost was not yet *given;* because that Jesus was not yet glorified.)"

2ⁿᵈ Corinthians 1:21-22 – "²¹ Now he which stablisheth us with you in Christ, and hath anointed us, *is* God; ²² **who hath also sealed us, and given the earnest of the Spirit in our hearts.**"

1ˢᵗ Corinthians 6:19-20 – "¹⁹ What? know ye not that **your body is the temple of the Holy Ghost** *which is* **in you**, which ye have of God, and ye are not your own? ²⁰ For ye are bought with a price: therefore glorify God in your body, and in your spirit, which are God's."

1ˢᵗ Corinthians 3:16 – "¹⁶ Know ye not that ye are the temple of God, **and** *that* **the Spirit of God dwelleth in you?**"

If you do not have the LORD Jesus Christ (the Holy Spirit of God) in your heart (inward man) then you are not a child of God.

Romans 8:9 – "[9] But ye are not in the flesh, but in the Spirit, if so be **that the Spirit of God dwell in you. Now if any man have not the Spirit of Christ, he is none of his.**"

Only those who had the Holy Spirit of God in their hearts at the time of the rapture were taken to be with the LORD Jesus Christ. This is my ballpark estimate on the number of those taken in the rapture: You will have a much better idea on this exact number since this event has already taken place. My numbers are only an estimate from late 2016 and may definitely be inaccurate. I extrapolated population growth numbers to about 2018 to 2023, just in case this world changing event was still a few more years in the future at the time of this writing – it is now November 1, 2016.

These numbers are based on my calculations using Wikipedia 2016 demographic data and running my own calculations and estimates based on my knowledge of the gospel influence in these nations. They were based on the religious demographics and the number of infants and young children. Note: every child reaches the age of reason at a different age – this is the age where they fully realize right from wrong and die spiritually because they partake of the tree of the knowledge of good and evil. I believe a typical child reaches this age at around 5 or 6 years. These account for the infants and young children raptured in the table (these numbers do not count the children in the womb at the time of the rapture as these are not in a nation's population numbers). My estimated number of people raptured (not including those in the womb) is as follows based on a world-wide population of approximately **8 Billion** before the rapture:

Country	Estimated Number of People Raptured - Adults and Older Children	Estimated Number of People Raptured - Infants and Young Children	Estimated Total Number of People Raptured (Vanished)	Population Remaining in Each Country immediately after Rapture
The USA	33,718,000	24,871,155	58,589,155	276,657,094
Brazil	7,733,880	15,589,357	23,323,237	186,676,763
Mexico	5,156,250	11,428,571	16,584,821	108,415,179
Russia	3,915,000	11,633,849	15,548,849	134,451,151
Philippians	4,224,000	12,357,143	16,581,143	89,809,140
Nigeria	5,750,125	27,928,571	33,678,696	151,321,304
China	4,800,300	68,450,125	73,250,425	1,326,749,575
India	7,239,375	117,901,758	125,141,133	1,304,858,867
Ethiopia	4,484,139	15,105,106	19,589,245	81,456,755
DR Congo	4,166,400	17,216,000	21,382,400	62,617,600
Rest of the World	24,165,820	400,328,204	424,494,024	3,837,555,298
World Totals	105,353,289	722,563,590	827,916,879	7,172,083,121

This table raises several questions. First why did so many infants and young children get raptured? The answer to this is simple: based on the scriptures these children were covered by the atonement of Jesus Christ (He died for all). Until such time as these children spiritually partake of the tree of the knowledge of good and evil and reach what I call "the age of reason", they were spiritually under the atonement of the LORD Jesus Christ.

The Full Atonement of the LORD Jesus Christ Covers the Original Sin of All Human Beings and Resulted in the Rapture of these Young Ones!

Matthew 23:37 – "³⁷ O Jerusalem, Jerusalem, *thou* that killest the prophets, and stonest them which are sent unto thee, how often **would I have** gathered thy children together, even as a hen gathereth her chickens under *her* wings, **and ye would not!**"

Obviously Jesus wanted to gather the Jewish people together and they would not have any part of it at His first coming. They rejected their Messiah! The primary reason for the rapture and the Seven Year Tribulation Period is a sign to turn the Jewish people in mass toward the LORD Jesus Christ as the Messiah, their Saviour!

John 1:9 – "⁹ *That* was the true Light, which lighteth **every man that cometh into the world.**"

This is clearly a **full atonement** as it applies to every man ever conceived.

John 3:16 – "¹⁶ For God so loved **the world**, that he gave his only begotten Son, that **whosoever** believeth in him should not perish, but have everlasting life."

Again this speaks to a **full atonement.**

Hebrews 2:9 – "⁹ But we see Jesus, who was made a little lower than the angels for the suffering of death, crowned with glory and honour; that he by the grace of God **should taste death for every man.**"

Jesus tasted death for **every man.** Again this speaks to a full atonement.

Acts 17:30 – "³⁰ And the times of this ignorance God winked at; but now commandeth **all men every where** to repent:" This statement that God commands all men everywhere clearly speaks to a **full atonement.** Why would God command man to do something and then not give man the capability to do it? If He expects all men everywhere to repent he must have died for all men everywhere or this command makes absolutely no sense.

1ˢᵗ Timothy 2:1-15 – "¹ I exhort therefore, that, first of all, supplications, prayers, intercessions, *and* giving of thanks, be made for **all men;** ² for kings, and *for* all that are in authority; that we may lead a quiet and peaceable life in all godliness and honesty. ³ For this *is* good and acceptable in the sight of God our Saviour; ⁴ **who will have all men to be saved, and to come unto the knowledge of the truth.** ⁵ For *there is* one God, and one mediator between God and men, the man Christ Jesus; ⁶ **who gave himself a ransom for all,** to be testified in due time."

Titus 2:11 – "¹¹ For the **grace of God that bringeth salvation hath appeared to all men,**"

These are clear passages as it states that Jesus gave Himself a ransom for all and the grace of God that bringeth salvation hath appeared to all mankind. I will also explain this later, but this teaches a **full atonement.**

2nd Peter 3:9 – "⁹ The Lord is not slack concerning his promise, as some men count slackness; but is longsuffering to us-ward, **not willing that any should perish, but that all should come to repentance.**"

Based on this verse it is obvious God does not desire anyone to perish in hell. Once again this is a clear teaching on the **full atonement**.

1st John 2:2 – "² **And he is the propitiation for our sins: and not for ours only, but also for** *the sins of* **the whole world.**"

Revelation 22:17 – "¹⁷ And the Spirit and the bride say, Come. And let him that heareth say, Come. And let him that is athirst come. And **whosoever will, let him take the water of life freely.**"

Again, whosoever will, can come to Jesus Christ, which clearly teaches a full atonement. Is the atonement of Jesus Christ on the cross full or limited? Based on the Bible alone it is definitely a **full atonement**.

Some folks teach the total depravity of man and then claim to believe in a limited atonement (Jesus died for only the elect), yet the verse below says the exact opposite. If you believe judgement came **upon all men** than you must believe the free gift of salvation came **upon all men** to be scriptural. The "all" in both parts of this verse must mean "all". In short if you believe that original sin applies to all men then you must believe the full atonement applies to all men.

Romans 5:18 - "Therefore as by the offence of one judgment came **upon all men** to condemnation; even so by the righteousness of one the free gift came **upon all men** unto justification of life."

John 12:32 - "And I, if I be lifted up from the earth, will draw **all men** unto me."

Titus 2:11 - "For the grace of God that bringeth salvation hath appeared to **all men**,"

1st Timothy 4:10 - "For therefore we both labour and suffer reproach, because we trust in the living God, who is the Saviour of **all men**, specially of those that believe."

So are we to conclude that all people are born again and going to heaven? - Of course not! This goes against many scriptures. But all men, including someone as wicked as Adolf Hitler, had a taste of the grace of God that bringeth salvation in their infancy. If Adolf Hitler would have died before he partook of the tree of the knowledge of good and evil (before he knew right from wrong), he would have went to heaven **because of the grace of God; because of the full atonement of Jesus Christ on the cross of Calvary; because of the free gift of eternal life. The grace of God is much greater than his original sin (Romans 5:20) and this grace did appear to Adolf Hitler in his infancy (Titus 2:11).**

But the day came when Adolf Hitler did partake of the tree of knowledge of good and evil **and at that moment his soul died and he became guilty before a Holy God – his sin was imputed to him. At that point the only way for him to go to heaven was to get born again and receive the Lord Jesus Christ by faith as His personal Saviour.** Whether it is the law of creation (Romans 1:19-21), the law of conscience (Romans

2:14-15), or the law of commandments (Romans 7:7-8); sin is not imputed when there is no law. The Apostle Paul spoke of this time in his life as a young child before the law revealed his sinful condition in the book of Romans. Paul said he was alive without the law once.

Romans 7:9 - "For I **was alive** without the law **once**: but when **the commandment came, sin revived, and I died.**"

The Apostle Paul was alive once (before he reached the age of reason) because of the full atonement. As Adam and Eve, Paul had no knowledge of sin before he partook of the tree of the knowledge of good and evil, when the law showed him right from wrong. But once he partook of this tree the Apostle Paul instantly died spiritually and he had to then get born again if he wanted to go to heaven instead of hell.

John 3:3 - "Jesus answered and said unto him, Verily, verily, I say unto thee, Except a man be born again, he cannot see the kingdom of God."

Ephesians 2:8-9 - "For by grace are ye saved through faith; and that not of yourselves: it is the gift of God: Not of works, lest any man should boast."

How did David know that his little infant son was in heaven and he would see him again if limited atonement is true? He knew his son was in heaven because limited atonement is NOT true - it is NOT Biblical. The atonement of Jesus Christ on the cross is full and complete and not limited."

2nd Samuel 12:23 - "But now he is dead, wherefore should I fast? can I bring him back again? **I shall go to him, but he shall not return to me."**

Now to answer the original question again: Does the Full Atonement of the LORD Jesus Christ cover all original sin?

- **YES – the atonement of the LORD Jesus Christ covers all original sin of all human beings.**
- **But the day comes when most people reach the age of reason (this age may be different for different folks - someone with a serious case of Down's Syndrome or another birth defect may never reach the age of reason). When this day comes and a person knows right from wrong, the Bible calls it partaking of the tree of the knowledge of good and evil, and when this happens the soul of that person immediately dies. See the verses that follow:**

Genesis 2:16 - 17 – "[16] And the Lord God commanded the man, saying, Of every tree of the garden thou mayest freely eat: [17] but of the **tree of the knowledge of good and evil, thou shalt not eat of it: for in the day that thou eatest thereof thou shalt surely die.**

When people reach this age of reason and partake of the tree of the knowledge of good and evil, they immediately die (spiritually).

This explains why the infants and young children all vanished in the recent rapture – they had not yet partaken of the tree of the knowledge of good and evil and were covered by the **full atonement through the shed blood of the LORD Jesus Christ! Therefore they were raptured!**

If you have NOT been born again and trusted the LORD Jesus Christ (the Messiah (God the Son) - the Creator of the Universe) as your personal Saviour, I encourage you to fall on your face and believe/call on Him right here and right now for the salvation of your eternal soul! You will need Him over the next Seven Years to face these times of the most severe persecutions and hardships that have ever come upon the earth! Both the wrath of God and the wrath of Satan will be unleashed!

If you will NOT trust Jesus Christ right now to save you from your sinful condition, then you might as well put this book down and submit to the Antichrist and his world system – the rest of this book will be useless to you without the LORD Jesus Christ and His Holy Spirit living inside of you to guide you over the next Seven Years! See the verses below – will you repent and trust Him now – will you believe on Him alone right now for the forgiveness of your sins and the salvation of your eternal soul? Please I beg you to bow your head and call on Him by faith right now!

Romans 3:9-11 – "[9] What then? are we better *than they?* No, in no wise: for we have before proved both Jews and Gentiles, that they are all under sin; [10] as it is written, There is none righteous, no, not one: [11] there is none that understandeth, there is none that seeketh after God."

Romans 3:20-26 - "[20] Therefore by **the deeds of the law there shall no flesh be justified in his sight**: for by the law *is* the knowledge of sin. [21] But now the righteousness of God without the law is manifested, being witnessed by the law and the prophets; [22] even the righteousness of God *which is* by faith of

Jesus Christ unto all and upon all them that believe: for there is no difference: [23] for all have sinned, and come short of the glory of God; [24] being justified freely by his grace through the redemption that is in Christ Jesus: [25] whom God hath set forth *to be* **a propitiation through faith in his blood**, to declare his righteousness for the remission of sins that are past, through the forbearance of God; [26] to declare, *I say*, at this time his righteousness: that he might be just, and the justifier of him which believeth in Jesus."

Romans 5:8-12 – "[8] But God commendeth his love toward us, in that, while we were yet sinners, Christ died for us. [9] Much more then, being now justified by his blood, we shall be saved from wrath through him. [10] For if, when we were enemies, we were reconciled to God by the death of his Son, much more, being reconciled, we shall be saved by his life. [11] And not only *so*, but we also joy in God through our Lord Jesus Christ, by whom we have now received the atonement."

Acts 4:12 – "[12] Neither is there salvation in any other: for there is none other name under heaven given among men, whereby we must be saved."

Isaiah 53:5 – "[5] But he *was* wounded for our transgressions, *he was* bruised for our iniquities: the chastisement of our peace *was* upon him; and with his stripes we are healed."

John 14:6 – "[6] Jesus saith unto him, I am the way, the truth, and the life: no man cometh unto the Father, but by me."

Romans 10:8-13 – "[8] But what saith it? The word is nigh thee, *even* in thy mouth, and in thy heart: that is, the word of faith, which we preach; [9] that if thou shalt confess with thy mouth the

Lord Jesus, and shalt believe in thine heart that God hath raised him from the dead, thou shalt be saved. [10] For with the heart man believeth unto righteousness; and with the mouth confession is made unto salvation. [11] For the scripture saith, Whosoever believeth on him shall not be ashamed. [12] For there is no difference between the Jew and the Greek: for the same Lord over all is rich unto all that call upon him. [13] For whosoever shall call upon the name of the Lord shall be saved."

John 3:14-16 – "[14] And as Moses lifted up the serpent in the wilderness, even so must the Son of man be lifted up: [15] that whosoever believeth in him should not perish, but have eternal life. [16] For God so loved the world, that he gave his only begotten Son, that whosoever believeth in him should not perish, but have everlasting life."

John 3:36 – "[36] He that believeth on the Son hath everlasting life: and he that believeth not the Son shall not see life; but the wrath of God abideth on him."

Once again I beg you to call upon the LORD Jesus Christ (God the Son) by faith right now and trust Him alone (plus nothing, minus nothing) for the salvation of your eternal soul! Get born again today by trusting the pure gospel (the death, burial, and bodily resurrection of the virgin born LORD Jesus Christ) which is able to save you from eternal fire in hell and give you eternal life with Him forever!

John 3:3 – "[3] Jesus answered and said unto him, Verily, verily, I say unto thee, **Except a man be born again**, he cannot see the kingdom of God."

John 3:7 – "⁷ Marvel not that I said unto thee, **Ye must be born again**."

1ˢᵗ Corinthians 15:1-4 – "¹ Moreover, brethren, I declare unto you **the gospel which I preached unto you**, which also ye have received, and wherein ye stand; ² **by which also ye are saved**, if ye keep in memory what I preached unto you, unless ye have believed in vain. ³ For I delivered unto you first of all that which I also received, **how that Christ died for our sins according to the scriptures; ⁴ and that he was buried, and that he rose again the third day according to the scriptures**:"

Chapter 2: Four Keys to Reading/Interpreting Prophetic Scripture about Future Events

Real Time Update: 1300 Hours; November 4, 2016: The rapture (catching up) of all truly born again believers (redeemed saints) has not happened yet at this time of this writing – although I expect it very soon.

I am now even more convinced that Donald Trump will be the next President of the United States of America – more convinced than I was three days ago. Hillary Clinton is ahead in the polls, but they are tightening. The reason I am convinced has absolutely nothing to do with the polls, but is based on certain scriptures that relate to the United States of America during the Seven Year Tribulation Period. I will explain this later in this book. The Presidential Election is in four days on Tuesday November 8, 2016. If I am wrong on this I may have to relook some of these things. And make no mistake, I am fully aware that the LORD's ways are not my ways (Isaiah 55:9), and He is fully capable of raising up one leader and putting down another and He is fully capable of raising up one country and putting down another.

As we begin this discussion on how to survive the next Seven Years, I want to give you **four keys** to properly understanding the scriptures, especially the prophetic scriptures related to future events that will come upon the earth very quickly. Knowing what is going to happen next on God's timetable before it actually happens will be essential to your survival! And the one book that has never missed on a prediction of a future event is the word of God (the Holy Bible), often referred to as the scripture or scriptures. Every prophecy about the first coming of the LORD Jesus Christ was **fulfilled literally** just as it was foretold in the Old Testament. Therefore it is my belief that every prophecy related to the 2nd Coming of the LORD Jesus Christ and end time events **will be fulfilled literally** just as foretold! I fully realize that the LORD will often use descriptive language and parables to explain future events. But generally when He does use this type of language, **He will provide the exact literal meaning in the scriptures themselves**. He wants us to understand exactly what He is talking about. See the examples below from the book of Revelation:

Revelation 1:19-20 – "[19] Write the things which thou hast seen, and the things which are, **and the things which shall be hereafter**; [20] the mystery of the seven stars which thou sawest in my right hand, and the seven golden candlesticks. **The seven stars are the angels of the seven churches: and the seven candlesticks which thou sawest are the seven churches.**"

Revelation 7:13-17 – "[13] And one of the elders answered, saying unto me, **What are these which are arrayed in white robes? and whence came they?** [14] And I said unto him, **Sir, thou knowest.** And he said to me, **These are they which came out of great tribulation, and have washed their robes, and made them white in the blood of the Lamb.** [15] **Therefore are they before the throne of God, and serve him day and night in his temple: and he that sitteth on the throne shall dwell among them.** [16] They shall hunger no more, neither thirst any more; neither shall the sun light on them, nor any heat. [17] For the Lamb which is in the midst of the throne shall feed them, and shall lead them unto living fountains of waters: and God shall wipe away all tears from their eyes."

Revelation 17:1-18 – "¹And there came one of the seven angels which had the seven vials, and talked with me, saying unto me, Come hither; I will shew unto thee the judgment of the great whore that sitteth upon many waters: ² with whom the kings of the earth have committed fornication, and the inhabitants of the earth have been made drunk with the wine of her fornication. ³ So he carried me away in the spirit into the wilderness: and **I saw a woman sit upon a scarlet coloured beast, full of names of blasphemy, having seven heads and ten horns.** ⁴ And the woman was arrayed in purple and scarlet colour, and decked with gold and precious stones and pearls, having a golden cup in her hand full of abominations and filthiness of her fornication: ⁵ and upon her forehead *was* a name written, **MYSTERY, BABYLON THE GREAT, THE MOTHER OF HARLOTS AND ABOMINATIONS OF THE EARTH.** ⁶ And I saw the woman drunken with the blood of the saints, and with the blood of the martyrs of Jesus: and when I saw her, I wondered with great admiration.

⁷ And the angel said unto me, **Wherefore didst thou marvel? I will tell thee the mystery of the woman, and of the beast that carrieth her, which hath the seven heads and ten horns. ⁸ The beast that thou sawest was, and is not; and shall ascend out of the bottomless pit, and go into perdition: and they that dwell on the earth shall wonder, whose names were not written in the book of life from the foundation of the world, when they behold the beast that was, and is not, and yet is.** ⁹ And here *is* the mind which hath wisdom. **The seven heads are seven mountains, on which the woman sitteth. ¹⁰ And there are seven kings: five are fallen, and one is, *and* the other is not yet come; and when he cometh, he must continue a short space. ¹¹ And the beast that was, and is not, even he is the eighth, and is of the seven, and goeth**

into perdition. ¹² And the ten horns which thou sawest are ten kings, which have received no kingdom as yet; but receive power as kings one hour with the beast. ¹³ These have one mind, and shall give their power and strength unto the beast. ¹⁴ These shall make war with the Lamb, and the Lamb shall overcome them: for he is Lord of lords, and King of kings: and they that are with him *are* called, and chosen, and faithful.

¹⁵ And he saith unto me, the waters which thou sawest, where the whore sitteth, are peoples, and multitudes, and nations, and tongues. ¹⁶ And the ten horns which thou sawest upon the beast, these shall hate the whore, and shall make her desolate and naked, and shall eat her flesh, and burn her with fire. ¹⁷ For God hath put in their hearts to fulfil his will, and to agree, and give their kingdom unto the beast, until the words of God shall be fulfilled. ¹⁸ And the woman which thou sawest is that great city, which reigneth over the kings of the earth."

Wow! The LORD tells us exactly what He is talking about! The seven candlesticks are the seven churches. The seven candles are the angels of the seven churches. Those arrayed in White Robes are redeemed tribulation saints who are washed in the blood of the Lamb. They came out of the tribulation period so they are tribulation period saints - saved and then murdered during the tribulation period – hopefully you are now a tribulation saint (If you are not I encourage you to reread chapter 1 and trust the LORD Jesus Christ for the salvation of your soul right now)! The Beast in Revelation 17 is obviously the Antichrist who deceived the world with the false miracle of his false resurrection. The seven heads are the seven mountains where the woman, Mystery Babylon the Great, sitteth. New

York City is the current location of the United Nations and reigneth over the kings of the earth. The ten horns are ten kings with no kingdom yet, but they receive power by spending one hour with the Beast (the Antichrist). And the waters where the woman sitteth are peoples, multitudes, nations, and tongues – it sounds like that MYSTERY BABYLON THE GREAT is a melting pot superpower nation with many different peoples in her midst.

I may not be right on every detail, but I promise you that when you read the LORD's descriptions of John's vision **literally** you have a much better chance of the proper interpretation of the scriptures! So that brings us to the first key to understanding future events in the Bible:

KEY # 1 – UNLESS THE CONTEXT CLEARLY DICTATES OTHERWISE, ALWAYS INTERPRET THE SCRIPTURES LITERALLY! DO NOT OVER ALLEGORIZE OR OVER SPIRITUALIZE THE SCRIPTURES FROM THE PLAIN MEANING THAT GOD INTENDED.

The LORD almost always lets us know when He is telling a parable or using descriptive/symbolic language to describe a literal event. Therefore if the LORD does not tell us that something described by Him represents something else (i.e. the seven candlesticks are the seven churches), then always interpret the scriptures literally just as they were written. For example the 1000 years described in Revelation chapter 20 is a literal 1000 year reign of the LORD Jesus Christ on the earth! Do not try to allegorize or symbolize the scriptures unless the LORD clearly explains the symbol in the scriptures themselves or the context totally leads differently. Jesus Christ did not write Revelation to confuse us, but to give us a clear understanding of future events before they happen!

The literal interpretation of the Bible and future end time events will open up the scriptures to you in a way that you have never seen them before. DO NOT look for secret or hidden meanings, but always accept the plain sense, literal reading/meaning of the passage unless context absolutely dictates otherwise!

The literal reading and interpretation of the Bible is <u>KEY #1</u> to understanding future end time events! That brings us to the second key to understanding future events – many Christians at the time of this writing (pre-rapture) miss this key – it is a common mistake made by many people.

<u>KEY #2</u> – NEVER REPLACE ISRAEL (THE JEWISH PEOPLE) WITH THE CHURCH (BORN AGAIN REDEEMED BELIEVERS) AND NEVER REPLACE THE CHURCH WITH ISRAEL! THIS IS CALLED REPLACEMENT THEOLOGY. DO NOT USE REPLACEMENT THEOLOGY WHEN INTERPRETING FUTURE EVENTS IN THE BIBLE!

Those that practice replacement theology will often explain that they are not practicing it, but when you dig a little deeper to what they are saying that is exactly what they are doing. There are certain promises and dispensations related to the nation of Israel and there are certain promises related to the bride of Christ, the church (Ephesians 5). Please do not get them confused. Much false doctrine originates because believers do not properly divide the Word of Truth, especially in this area.

2nd Timothy 2:15 – "[15] Study to shew thyself approved unto God, a workman that needeth not to be ashamed, **rightly dividing the word of truth**."

If the rapture has already taken place and the peace treaty has been signed with the Antichrist and the nation of Israel, then you are in the Seven Year Tribulation Period right now. It started with the signing of this Seven Year peace treaty. This is a time where both the wrath of Satan and the wrath of God is unleashed on the earth with the primary purpose of turning the Jewish people in mass toward a saving knowledge of the Messiah, the LORD Jesus Christ! Many more people in addition to the Jews are redeemed during the tribulation period (most surely many millions of Gentiles will be saved during Daniel's 70th Week). These saved Gentiles will both greatly suffer on the earth during this Seven Years and greatly benefit in eternity from God's dealings with the Jews. But all that being said, the main purpose of the great turmoil/destruction on the earth during this period is to reach the LORD's chosen people - the nation of Israel!

Even though the teachings in all the scriptures have applications to all believers, there are certain promises (in their Bible context) that were made specifically for the Jewish people. We can see this in many Old Testament passages and in Paul's gospel to the Romans in chapters 9, 10, and 11. Let us look at chapter 11 in its entirety so you are aware of what I am saying with regard to the nation of Israel:

Romans 11:1-36 – "[1] I say then, Hath God cast away his people? God forbid. For I also am an Israelite, of the seed of Abraham, *of* the tribe of Benjamin. [2] God hath not cast away his people which he foreknew.** Wot ye not what the scripture saith of Elias? how he maketh intercession to God against Israel, saying, [3] Lord, they have killed thy prophets, and digged down thine altars; and I am left alone, and they seek my life. [4] But what saith the answer of God unto him? I have reserved to myself seven thousand men, who have not bowed the knee to *the image of* Baal. [5] Even so then at this present time also there is a remnant according to the election of grace. [6] And if by grace, then *is it* no more of works: otherwise grace is no more grace. But if *it be* of works, then is it no more grace: otherwise work is no more work.

[7] What then? Israel hath not obtained that which he seeketh for; but the election hath obtained it, and the rest were blinded [8] (according as it is written, God hath given them the spirit of slumber, eyes that they should not see, and ears that they should not hear;) unto this day. [9] And David saith, Let their table be made a snare, and a trap, and a stumblingblock, and a recompence unto them: [10] let their eyes be darkened, that they may not see, and bow down their back alway. **[11] I say then, Have they stumbled that they should fall? God forbid: but *rather* through their fall salvation *is come* unto the Gentiles, for to provoke them to jealousy. [12] Now if the fall of them *be* the riches of the world, and the diminishing of them the riches of the Gentiles; how much more their fulness?**

[13] For I speak to you Gentiles, inasmuch as I am the apostle of the Gentiles, I magnify mine office: [14] if by any means I may provoke to emulation *them which are* my flesh, and might save some of them. **[15] For if the casting away of them *be* the reconciling of the world, what *shall* the receiving *of them be,* but life from the dead? [16] For if the firstfruit *be* holy, the lump *is* also *holy:* and if the root *be* holy, so *are* the branches.** [17] And if some of the branches be broken off, and

thou, being a wild olive tree, wert graffed in among them, and with them partakest of the root and fatness of the olive tree; [18] boast not against the branches. But if thou boast, thou bearest not the root, but the root thee. [19] Thou wilt say then, The branches were broken off, that I might be graffed in. [20] Well; because of unbelief they were broken off, and thou standest by faith. Be not highminded, but fear: [21] for if God spared not the natural branches, *take heed* lest he also spare not thee. [22] Behold therefore the goodness and severity of God: on them which fell, severity; but toward thee, goodness, if thou continue in *his* goodness: otherwise thou also shalt be cut off. [23] **And they also, if they abide not still in unbelief, shall be graffed in: for God is able to graff them in again. [24] For if thou wert cut out of the olive tree which is wild by nature, and wert graffed contrary to nature into a good olive tree: how much more shall these, which be the natural *branches*, be graffed into their own olive tree?**

[25] **For I would not, brethren, that ye should be ignorant of this mystery, lest ye should be wise in your own conceits; that blindness in part is happened to Israel, until the fulness of the Gentiles be come in. [26] And so all Israel shall be saved: as it is written, There shall come out of Sion the Deliverer, and shall turn away ungodliness from Jacob: [27] for this *is* my covenant unto them, when I shall take away their sins.** [28] As concerning the gospel, *they are* enemies for your sakes: but as touching the election, *they are* beloved for the fathers' sakes. [29] **For the gifts and calling of God *are* without repentance.** [30] For as ye in times past have not believed God, yet have now obtained mercy through their unbelief: [31] even so have these also now not believed, that through your mercy they also may obtain mercy. [32] For God hath concluded them all in unbelief, that he might have mercy

upon all. [33] O the depth of the riches both of the wisdom and knowledge of God! how unsearchable *are* his judgments, and his ways past finding out! [34] For who hath known the mind of the Lord? or who hath been his counsellor? [35] Or who hath first given to him, and it shall be recompensed unto him again? [36] For of him, and through him, and to him, *are* all things: to whom *be* glory for ever. Amen."

What a wonderful chapter about the Jewish people of the nation of Israel. God is going to graft the natural branches (the Jewish people) back into their own olive tree (the LORD Jesus Christ) during the tribulation period! Christian, if you want the LORD's best blessings during this time of great destruction, then you do everything possible to be a friend and help to the Jewish people in the coming days of the Seven Year Tribulation Period. They are the apple of God's eye and during this time they will be the target of Satan's strongest attacks – especially during the last three and half years of the tribulation period. This is called the time of Jacob's Trouble. Satan hates and attacks all Christians during this period, but he hates and attacks Jewish Christians the most because they are the apple of God's eye!

Every single promise made by God to the nation of Israel will be fulfilled literally as He foretold! Those unconditional national promises made to the Jewish people that have not yet been fulfilled, will be literally fulfilled in full during the 1000 year reign of the LORD Jesus Christ on this earth! Look what the Bible says in the book of Zechariah about mortals during the millennial reign of Jesus on this earth. Ten men will follow one Jew, because the LORD is with him.

Zechariah 8:23 – "²³ Thus saith the Lord of hosts; In those days it shall come to pass, that ten men shall take hold out of all languages of the nations, even shall take hold of the skirt of him that is a Jew, saying, We will go with you: for we have heard that God is with you."

Do not spiritualize this verse away with replacement theology. This specifically talks about the distinction between the nation of Israel and other nations during the millennial reign of Jesus on the earth and how the Jew is greatly honored during this period - other nations are judged going into the 1000 year reign based on their treatment of the Jews during the Seven Year Tribulation Period (Matthew chapter 25).

Real Time Update: 0035 Hours; November 27, 2016: The rapture (catching up) of all truly born again believers (redeemed saints) has not happened yet at this time of this writing – although I expect it very soon.

As I predicted Donald Trump won the Presidential Election on November 8, 2016 and will be the next President of the United States of America. He ended up with 306 electoral votes and only needed 270 electoral votes to become President. He will be inaugurated as the next President in January 2017. Everyone in the news media and all the polling data (with very few exceptions) expected Hillary Clinton to be the next President of the United States. Early in the evening she was given a 95% chance of winning the election by many of the so called experts. Donald Trump ended up winning all of the states he had to win and upset her in the states of Michigan, Pennsylvania, and Wisconsin, securing all of their electoral votes and winning the election.

*The reason that I totally expected this is because I am 99.9%
certain based on the scriptures (Jeremiah chapters 50 & 51,
Revelation chapters 17 and 18, along with other passages) that
the United States of America is the superpower nation, **Mystery
Babylon the Great**, which is completely destroyed in one hour
near the very end of the Seven Year Tribulation Period, just
before the Battle of Armageddon. I will explain this in much
greater detail in chapter 4 of this book. Donald Trump's
campaign theme was: **"Make America Great Again"** and I
believe from an economic perspective that he will be successful
in this endeavor. Morally, I believe that America will continue
to decline at a rapid rate, but economically I believe she will
recover and remain a superpower. If America is **Mystery
Babylon the Great** then she still has to be great and she still
has to be a superpower even after the rapture. The rapture
(which should have already occurred) is before the Seven Year
Tribulation Period, during which Mystery Babylon the Great is
destroyed as part of God's judgment – See my book: "Why I
Believe in a Pre-Tribulation Rapture". If Hillary Clinton would
have been elected I believe that America would have continued
to decline both economically and morally and would likely have
not existed as a superpower nation at the time of the rapture,
and at the time of the follow on Seven Year Tribulation Period.*

*I have some deep concerns by the attitude of many of my
Christian brothers and sisters in Christ over the recent United
States election. It seems like they are putting more trust in
Donald Trump and the Republicans to turn this country around
than in the LORD Jesus Christ. Their hope was in the election
and not in Jesus! I believe many of them have the same attitude
that Hezekiah did when Isaiah told him in Isaiah 39 that his
offspring would be carried away captive into Babylon and be
eunuchs in the palace of the king of Babylon, but Judah would*

---

be safe in his lifetime. Instead of mourning for his posterity and the judgment that was to come upon them, Hezekiah said: "Good is the word of the LORD…" Though Hezekiah was a righteous king, he was more concerned about himself and what happened in his lifetime than he was about what happen to the future generations and to his nation.

This is the attitude of most Christians today – they are fine with future judgment as long as the judgment of America does not come in their lifetime before the rapture. My question to these believers is this: **What about the millions in America not saved and who are left behind at the rapture? What about the millions in America who believe the lie of Satan after the rapture? What about the millions in America who take the mark of the Beast during the second half of the tribulation period? What about the millions in America who remain unregenerate and are destroyed by the nuclear attack in one hour by the Beast and the 10 nations that get their power with the Beast (this is the judgment of God, but carried out by the heathen, for the wickedness of America during the tribulation period)?**

Enough with the real time update and back to the book. We have already discussed the first two keys to understanding prophecy and specifically to understanding the book of Revelation. They are as follows:

KEY # 1 – UNLESS THE CONTEXT CLEARLY DICTATES OTHERWISE, ALWAYS INTERPRET THE SCRIPTURES LITERALLY! DO NOT ALLEGORIZE OR SPIRITUALIZE THE SCRIPTURES FROM THE PLAIN MEANING THAT GOD INTENDED.

KEY #2 – NEVER REPLACE ISRAEL (THE JEWISH PEOPLE) WITH THE CHURCH (BORN AGAIN REDEEMED BELIEVERS) AND NEVER REPLACE THE CHURCH WITH ISRAEL! THIS IS CALLED REPLACEMENT THEOLOGY. DO NOT USE REPLACEMENT THEOLOGY WHEN INTERPRETING FUTURE EVENTS IN THE BIBLE!

That brings us to the third key:

KEY #3 – ALWAYS ALLOW THE HOLY SPIRIT TO TEACH YOU THINGS THAT ARE TO COME AND TO GIVE YOU WISDOM REGARDING THE FUTURE EVENTS PROPHESIED IN THE BIBLE!

See the verses that follow related to this third key:

John 14:26 – "²⁶ But the Comforter, *which is* **the Holy Ghost**, whom the Father will send in my name, **he shall teach you all things**, and bring all things to your remembrance, whatsoever I have said unto you."

John 16:13 – "¹³ Howbeit when he, **the Spirit of truth**, is come, he will guide you into all truth: for he shall not speak of himself; but whatsoever he shall hear, *that* shall he speak: and **he will shew you things to come**."

James 1:5 – "⁵ If any of you **lack wisdom**, let him **ask of God**, that giveth to all *men* liberally, and upbraideth not; **and it shall be given him**."

1ˢᵗ Thessalonians 5:1-8 – "¹But of the times and the seasons, brethren, ye have no need that I write unto you. ² For yourselves know perfectly that **the day of the Lord so cometh as a thief in the night**. [3] For when they shall say, Peace and safety; then sudden destruction cometh upon them, as travail upon a woman with child; and they shall not escape. [4] **But ye, brethren, are not in darkness, that that day should overtake you as a thief.** [5] **Ye are all the children of light, and the children of the day: we are not of the night, nor of darkness.** [6] **Therefore let us not sleep, as** *do* **others; but let us watch and be sober.** [7] For they that sleep sleep in the night; and they that be drunken are drunken in the night. [8] **But let us, who are of the day, be sober, putting on the breastplate of faith and love; and for an helmet, the hope of salvation."**

1st Corinthians 2:9-10 – "[9] But as it is written, Eye hath not seen, nor ear heard, neither have entered into the heart of man, the things which God hath prepared for them that love him. [10] **But God hath revealed** *them* **unto us by his Spirit: for the Spirit searcheth all things, yea, the deep things of God."**

The day of the Lord referred to in 1st Thessalonians includes the entire Seven Year Tribulation Period and this day will come as a thief in the night because the initial domino that must fall to kick off this event is the rapture of the church age saints. I am guessing that if you are now reading this book, that the rapture has already happened, and many millions have already disappeared off the face of the earth. Even though the Seven Year Tribulation Period has recently just begun, none of these future events during this period in which you are now living have to catch you by surprise - if you are now born again and have recently become a tribulation saint. You are now a child of light and have the Holy Spirit of God inside of you along with the Holy Scriptures – therefore none of the events that are about to come upon the entire earth have to surprise you or catch you unprepared!

You can predict what future event will happen next based on the word of God (the Bible) as the Holy Ghost of God now living inside of you teaches you! To be able to know future events before they happen is a **HUGE WEAPON** in your favor during the tribulation period! You and your family can be prepared for the destruction that is about to come upon the entire earth. Be sure NOT to take a hermit's approach during this period, thinking only of yourself and your family – you must help the people of the nation of Israel and fellow tribulation saints! Surely there will be times of hiding and times of running, but these times of tribulation are also a great opportunity for service to the LORD Jesus Christ, His tribulation saints, and His Jewish remnant from the nation of Israel! There will be certain judgments directly upon those that are NOT redeemed by the blood of the LAMB (the LORD Jesus Christ). During these judgments on the lost you may have a short reprieve and a greater opportunity to serve the LORD Jesus Christ and serve others (especially Jewish people and newly saved tribulation Saints (both Jews and Gentiles alike)).

Be careful who you trust, but do not just hide away in fear during the tribulation period! There will be much death on the earth during these Seven Years – death caused by man and directly from the wrath of God and the wrath of Satan! Many of you will die for your faith in the LORD Jesus Christ! Many of your own family members will turn you in to the authorities where many of you will surely be executed for your faith. Do not lose hope for the LORD will be with you and grant you an eternal home in heaven with Him, along with a special place in His soon to come millennial kingdom on the earth.

Now to the fourth key which relates specifically to the first 3 ½ years of the tribulation period:

<u>KEY #4</u> – LISTEN INTENLY AND OBEY THE 144,000 CHOSEN JEWISH WITNESSES AND GOD'S TWO SPECIAL PROPHETS FROM JERUSALEM (MOST LIKELY ELIJAH AND MOSES) DURING THE FIRST HALF (3 ½ YEARS) OF THE TRIBULATION PERIOD!

Another place to get direction during this time of great trouble is from the 144,000 chosen Jewish witnesses and the two special witnesses (believed to be Elijah and Moses) at Jerusalem. You can trust everything they tell you as gospel truth without any mixture of error, but be aware of false prophets and imitators. See the following verses describing the ministry of these special prophets of God so you know for certain who they are and the purpose of their ministry during the first half of the tribulation period – 3 ½ years (1260 days). If someone claims to be one of these special prophets and does not fit the Bible description, then DO NOT trust them. These 144,000 chosen ones are Jewish male virgins – 12,000 from each tribe of Israel – see the verses that follow:

The 144,000 Jewish Witnesses

Revelation 7:1-8 – " [1]And after these things I saw four angels standing on the four corners of the earth, holding the four winds of the earth, that the wind should not blow on the earth, nor on the sea, nor on any tree. [2] And I saw another angel ascending from the east, having the seal of the living God: and he cried with a loud voice to the four angels, to whom it was given to hurt the earth and the sea, [3] saying, **Hurt not the earth, neither the sea, nor the trees, till we have sealed the servants of our**

God in their foreheads. ⁴ And I heard the number of them which were sealed: *and there were* sealed an hundred *and* forty *and* four thousand of all the tribes of the children of Israel. ⁵ Of the tribe of Juda *were* sealed twelve thousand. Of the tribe of Reuben *were* sealed twelve thousand. Of the tribe of Gad *were* sealed twelve thousand. ⁶ Of the tribe of Aser *were* sealed twelve thousand. Of the tribe of Nepthalim *were* sealed twelve thousand. Of the tribe of Manasses *were* sealed twelve thousand. ⁷ Of the tribe of Simeon *were* sealed twelve thousand. Of the tribe of Levi *were* sealed twelve thousand. Of the tribe of Issachar *were* sealed twelve thousand. ⁸ Of the tribe of Zabulon *were* sealed twelve thousand. Of the tribe of Joseph *were* sealed twelve thousand. Of the tribe of Benjamin *were* sealed twelve thousand."

Revelation 14:1-5 – "¹ And I looked, and, lo, a Lamb stood on the mount Sion, **and with him an hundred forty *and* four thousand, having his Father's name written in their foreheads.** ² And I heard a voice from heaven, as the voice of many waters, and as the voice of a great thunder: and I heard the voice of harpers harping with their harps: ³ and they sung as it were a new song before the throne, and before the four beasts, and the elders: **and no man could learn that song but the hundred *and* forty *and* four thousand, which were redeemed from the earth.** ⁴ **These are they which were not defiled with women; for they are virgins. These are they which follow the Lamb whithersoever he goeth. These were redeemed from among men,** *being* **the firstfruits unto God and to the Lamb.** ⁵ And in their mouth was found no guile: for they are without fault before the throne of God."

I am going to tell you what I believe about these 144,000 virgin, male, Jewish witnesses:

1) **I believe they immediately get saved right after the rapture of the church age saints and are sealed by God to be His special appointed witnesses during the first 3 ½ years of the tribulation period on the earth.** I believe Revelation chapter 7 and Revelation 14 give us some clues to the identity of these that are sealed in their foreheads at the very beginning of the tribulation period.

    a. I believe the LORD Jesus Christ is never without a witness on the earth. He was on the earth 2000 years ago. After His resurrection when He was glorified He gave His Holy Spirit to indwell all believers (John 20:21-22).

    b. When all believers were raptured, the Holy Spirit (who indwells all believers) was temporarily removed when the body of Christ disappeared from the earth; or at least His influence through believers (2nd Thessalonians 2:7). But immediately after the rapture these 144,000 Jewish witnesses trust Christ as the Saviour and also receive the indwelling Holy Ghost (Mark 13:11). The reason I believe this is as follows:

        ▪ I believe Revelation chapter 7 actually occurs before or at the same exact time as the seal judgements in Revelation chapter 6, even though John sees the vision of chapter 7 afterwards. The reason I say this is because the angel with the seals cried to the four angels: "Hurt not the earth, neither the sea, nor the trees, till we have sealed the servants of our God in their foreheads." – Revelation 7:3; and in revelation chapter 6 the LORD does hurt the earth with the great earthquake at the 6th seal judgment – Revelation 6:12-17.

- I believe Revelation chapter 7 is like an interlude to describe for us the ministry of the 144,000 Jewish witnesses. Both chapters 6 and 7 describe for us the same group of early tribulation saints – consisting of the multitudes of people saved and murdered early in the tribulation period. I believe these early tribulation saints are primarily led to faith in Christ by these 144,000 Jewish witnesses.

- Also in Revelation 14:4 the scriptures call these 144,000 the "first fruits" – specifically it says: "These were redeemed from among men, *being* **the firstfruits unto God and to the Lamb**."

2) **I believe this 144,000 cause great revival across the globe and are responsible for multitudes of Jews and Gentiles alike trusting Christ as their personal Saviour during the early days of the tribulation period.** This is alluded to in Revelation 7:9-17 right after the 144,000 Jewish witnesses are introduced to us. Here we read about multitudes that get saved and are murdered for their new found faith, early in the tribulation period. I

believe that these 144,000 Jewish witnesses are personally responsible for this mass revival across the globe. See the verses that follow:

Revelation 7:9-17 – "⁹ After this I beheld, and, lo, **a great multitude, which no man could number, of all nations, and kindreds, and people, and tongues, stood before the throne, and before the Lamb, clothed with white robes**, and palms in their hands; ¹⁰ and cried with a loud voice, saying, Salvation to our God which sitteth upon the throne, and unto the Lamb. ¹¹ And all the angels stood round about the throne, and *about* the elders and the four beasts, and fell before the throne on their faces, and worshipped God, ¹² saying, Amen: Blessing, and glory, and wisdom, and thanksgiving, and honour, and power, and might, *be* unto our God for ever and ever. Amen.

¹³ And one of the elders answered, saying unto me, **What are these which are arrayed in white robes? and whence came they?** ¹⁴ And I said unto him, Sir, thou knowest. And he said to me, **These are they which came out of great tribulation, and have washed their robes, and made them white in the blood of the Lamb**. ¹⁵ Therefore are they before the throne of God, and serve him day and night in his temple: and he that sitteth on the throne shall dwell among them. ¹⁶ They shall hunger no more, neither thirst any more; neither shall the sun light on them, nor any heat. ¹⁷ For the Lamb which is in the midst of the throne shall feed them, and shall lead them unto living fountains of waters: and God shall wipe away all tears from their eyes."

3) Though this is not stated directly, **I believe these 144,000 witnesses are killed by the Antichrist (the beast) and his False Prophet at the halfway point of the 7-year tribulation period.** I believe this because the next description of the 144,000 Jewish witnesses seems to place them in heaven before the throne of God at the halfway point of the tribulation period. See the scripture reference that follows:

Revelation 14:1-5 – "[1]And I looked, and, lo, a Lamb stood on the mount Sion, and with him **an hundred forty *and* four thousand, having his Father's name written in their foreheads.** [2] And I heard a voice from heaven, as the voice of many waters, and as the voice of a great thunder: and I heard the voice of harpers harping with their harps: [3] **and they sung as it were a new song before the throne, and before the four beasts, and the elders: and no man could learn that song but the hundred *and* forty *and* four thousand, which were redeemed from the earth**. [4] These are they which were not defiled with women; for they are virgins. These are they which follow the Lamb whithersoever he goeth. **These were redeemed from among men, *being* the firstfruits unto God and to the Lamb**. [5] And in their mouth was found no guile: for they are without fault before the throne of God."

The landmark of the halfway point of the Seven Year Tribulation Period is easily identified for us in the book of Revelation in chapters 11, 12, and 13. Revelation chapter 11 describes the ministry of the two witnesses (the two olive trees and the two candlesticks believed to be Elijah and Moses) during the first half of the tribulation, and the sounding of the seventh Trumpet at the halfway point of the Seven Year Tribulation Period.

Revelation chapter 12 summarizes a history of the Devil's battle against the nation of Israel and the LORD Jesus Christ, culminating with the final removal of Satan from heaven and his wrath poured out on God's people (especially on the children of Israel) during the last half of the tribulation.

Revelation chapter 13 describes the rise of the Antichrist (the Beast) along with the False Prophet (another Beast) and their supreme rule over the earth. The Antichrist is given power over God's people during the last 3 ½ years of the tribulation period.

All three of these chapters provide for us a landmark of the halfway point of the Seven Year Tribulation Period on the earth. Revelation chapter 11 describes for us the 1260 day preaching ministry (first half of the tribulation period) of the two witnesses at Jerusalem ending when they are killed by the Beast (the Antichrist) at the halfway point of the tribulation period. The holy city (Jerusalem) is given over to the Gentiles during the last half of the tribulation period to tread under foot for 42 months. No one is going to desecrate the holy temple at Jerusalem nor tread the city under foot while these two witnesses are still alive and working their miracles from Jerusalem during the first half of the tribulation. See the passage below:

Revelation 11:1-8 – "[1]And there was given me a reed like unto a rod: and the angel stood, saying, Rise, and measure the temple of God, and the altar, and them that worship therein. [2] But the court which is without the temple leave out, and measure it not; for it is given unto the Gentiles: **and the holy city shall they tread under foot <u>forty *and* two months</u>**. [3] And I will give *power* unto my two witnesses, **and they shall prophesy <u>a thousand two hundred *and* threescore days</u>, clothed in sackcloth.**

[4] These are the two olive trees, and the two candlesticks standing before the God of the earth. [5] **And if any man will hurt them, fire proceedeth out of their mouth, and devoureth their enemies: and if any man will hurt them, he must in this manner be killed. [6] These have power to shut heaven, that it rain not in the days of their prophecy: and have power over waters to turn them to blood, and to smite the earth with all plagues, as often as they will.** [7] And when they shall have finished their testimony, the beast that ascendeth out of the bottomless pit shall make war against them, and shall overcome them, and kill them. [8] And their dead bodies *shall lie* in the street of the great city, which spiritually is **called Sodom and Egypt, where also our Lord was crucified."**

I personally believe that the 144,000 Jewish Witnesses are also killed by the Antichrist (the Beast) at the halfway point of the Seven Year Tribulation Period. This is confirmed for us in Revelation 14 as already noted when we see these 144,000 singing a new song that only they could learn up in heaven (before the throne of God).

In Revelation chapter 13 we read how the Antichrist (the Beast) is given complete power over the saints and all people on the earth during the last 3 ½ years of the tribulation period.

Revelation 13:3-8 – "³ And I saw one of his heads as it were wounded to death; and his deadly wound was healed: and all the world wondered after the beast. ⁴ And they worshipped the dragon which gave power unto the beast: and they worshipped the beast, saying, Who *is* like unto the beast? who is able to make war with him? ⁵ And there was given unto him a mouth speaking great things and blasphemies; and **power was given unto him to continue <u>forty *and* two months</u>.** ⁶ And he opened his mouth in blasphemy against God, to blaspheme his name, and his tabernacle, and them that dwell in heaven. ⁷ **And it was given unto him to make war with the saints, and to overcome them: and power was given him over all kindreds, and tongues, and nations.** ⁸ And all that dwell upon the earth shall worship him, whose names are not written in the book of life of the Lamb slain from the foundation of the world."

See the quick chronological summary below of the many events at the midpoint of the Seven Year Tribulation Period on the earth.

A QUICK CHRONOLOGICAL SUMMARY OF REVELATION CHAPTERS 11, 12, & 13

- **The two prophets (Elijah and Moses) prophesy and work miracles for 1260 days from Jerusalem - the first half of the tribulation period.**

- The Beast (the Antichrist) works a false resurrection of a dead (most likely murdered) world leader and takes possession of the leader's body – he then precedes to kill God's two special prophets and to desecrate the temple of God (the Abomination of Desolation) at the halfway point of the tribulation period. At around this same time I believe the Antichrist is also given power over the 144,000 Jewish witnesses and has them also killed along with many other believers.

- Many of the nation of Israel flee from Jerusalem/Judea for their lives into the wilderness when they see the Abomination of Desolation where the Antichrist is revealed for who he is.

- The Seventh Trumpet sounds at the halfway point of the tribulation period, marking the beginning of the absolute rule of the Antichrist on the earth and the seven last vial judgments – this is called the third woe and marks the beginning of the last 3 ½ years of the tribulation period. This is a time of rejoicing up in heaven, because the Devil is permanently cast out of heaven never to return (Revelation 12:7-10). But it is a time of great woe on the earth because the Devil is now on the earth with great wrath because he knows his time is short (Revelation 12:12-17). The sounding of the seventh trumpet marks the beginning of the end for the Devil, the Antichrist, and the False Prophet.

- The Beast (the Antichrist), the Dragon (the Devil), and the other Beast (the False Prophet) take total

control of the earth and force worship of the Beast
during the last half of the tribulation period, killing
all who refuse to worship him or take the mark of the
Beast. I believe that God shortens the length of each
day before this time period on the earth so it passes
much more quickly and some of the tribulation saints
are able to survive to see the glorious appearing of
Jesus (Matthew 24:22 and Revelation 8:12).

At the halfway point of the tribulation period,
immediately after the death of God's two special
prophets at Jerusalem and these 144,000 chosen Jewish
witnesses, the LORD assigns three angels to go across
the globe declaring three messages to the inhabitants of
the earth:

1. Preaching the everlasting gospel and encouraging
   worship of the true God!

2. Warning of the coming destruction of the superpower
   nation – Mystery Babylon the Great (the United States
   of America)!

3. Warning the inhabitants of the earth NOT to worship
   and take the mark of the Beast!

See the verses that follow in Revelation chapter 14 after
the 144,000 witnesses are shown up in heaven before the
throne of God:

Revelation 14:6-12 – "[6] **And I saw another angel fly in
the midst of heaven, having the everlasting gospel to
preach unto them that dwell on the earth**, and to every

nation, and kindred, and tongue, and people, [7] saying with a loud voice, Fear God, and give glory to him; for the hour of his judgment is come: and worship him that made heaven, and earth, and the sea, and the fountains of waters.

[8] And **there followed another angel, saying, Babylon is fallen, is fallen, that great city, because she made all nations drink of the wine of the wrath of her fornication.**

[9] And **the third angel followed them, saying with a loud voice, If any man worship the beast and his image, and receive *his* mark in his forehead, or in his hand,** [10] the same shall drink of the wine of the wrath of God, which is poured out without mixture into the cup of his indignation; and he shall be tormented with fire and brimstone in the presence of the holy angels, and in the presence of the Lamb: [11] and the smoke of their torment ascendeth up for ever and ever: and they have no rest day nor night, who worship the beast and his image, and whosoever receiveth the mark of his name. [12] Here is the patience of the saints: here *are* they that keep the commandments of God, and the faith of Jesus.

Before I move to the next chapter and describe an event I call: The Purging of the Early Tribulation Saints, I want to review again the four keys to reading/interpreting prophetic scripture about future events and then provide you :

KEY # 1 – UNLESS THE CONTEXT CLEARLY DICTATES OTHERWISE, ALWAYS INTERPRET THE SCRIPTURES LITERALLY! DO NOT ALLEGORIZE OR

SPIRITUALIZE THE SCRIPTURES FROM THE PLAIN MEANING THAT GOD INTENDED.

KEY #2 – NEVER REPLACE ISRAEL (THE JEWISH PEOPLE) WITH THE CHURCH (BORN AGAIN REDEEMED BELIEVERS) AND NEVER REPLACE THE CHURCH WITH ISRAEL! THIS IS CALLED REPLACEMENT THEOLOGY. DO NOT USE REPLACEMENT THEOLOGY WHEN INTERPRETING FUTURE EVENTS IN THE BIBLE! RIGHTLY DIVIDE THE SCRIPTURES!

KEY #3 – ALWAYS ALLOW THE HOLY SPIRIT TO TEACH YOU THINGS THAT ARE TO COME AND TO GIVE YOU WISDOM REGARDING THE FUTURE EVENTS PROPHESIED IN THE BIBLE!

KEY #4 – LISTEN INTENLY AND OBEY THE 144,000 CHOSEN JEWISH WITNESSES AND GOD'S TWO SPECIAL PROPHETS FROM JERUSALEM (MOST LIKELY ELIJAH AND MOSES) DURING THE FIRST HALF (3 ½ YEARS) OF THE TRIBULATION PERIOD!

Chapter 3: The First Purging - Extermination of the Early Tribulation Saints

Real Time Update: 1715 Hours; April 19, 2017: I have not spent a lot of time on this book recently, but I decided to begin writing again this afternoon. The rapture (catching up) of all truly born again believers (redeemed saints) has not happened yet at the time of this writing – although I expect it very soon.

A recent current event:

The United States has officially attacked Syria
Zack Beauchamp and Yochi Dreazen with Vox on April 6, 2017

*"The United States has just intentionally **bombed a Syrian regime target** for the first time since the country's civil war began in 2011. So far, it has been a limited cruise missile strike targeting one Syrian airbase, causing an as-yet-unknown number of casualties.*

"Dozens of Tomahawks were launched against a single Syrian regime airfield," a Department of Defense official told Vox.

*The decision to attack was a direct reaction to the Syrian regime's Tuesday gas attack that claimed 85 lives, including about two dozen children. Images of the Syrians who suffocated to death seemed to shock President Trump, who **spoke** Wednesday of the "beautiful little babies" killed in the attack, which he described as "an affront to humanity."*

RELATED

President Trump speaks after ordering attack on Syria

*Trump went even further Thursday, **telling** reporters that "something should happen" to Syrian President Bashar al-Assad because of his responsibility for the attack. Secretary of State Rex Tillerson, meanwhile, **said** Assad would have "no role" governing Syria in the future and that "steps are underway" for a US-led international push to remove him.*

http://www.vox.com/world/2017/4/6/15214758/us-syria-assad-bomb-cruise-missile

Enough of the real time updates. The purpose of this chapter is to discuss the purging (extermination) of millions of newly redeemed tribulation saints during the early part of the Seven Year Tribulation Period (Daniel's 70th Week). I want to make a few statements here to set the stage by describing the events that will lead up to the mass murder of the newly saved tribulation saints.

First, the rapture has just happened and according to my estimates (see page 6 of this book) approximately **828 Million** people have just disappeared off the face of the earth. An event of this magnitude has never happened in human history! Additionally, the bulk of these 828 Million (approximately **723 Million**) are infants and young children – there is hardly a family on the globe that is not touched by this event.

I am not sure where you are at in the current Seven Year Tribulation Period, but something will or has already happened immediately after the rapture on two fronts, and you either have already experienced it or are about to experience it.

Front 1 – Mass Revival: The 144,000 Jewish witnesses and the two prophets at Jerusalem (Elijah and Moses in my opinion) have preached the truth of the Rapture & the gospel of Jesus

Christ to millions (maybe billions across the globe) and mass revival has occurred or is presently occurring. The two prophets at Jerusalem are probably on the internet and can be heard by anyone who wants to hear them. The 144,000 Jewish witnesses are traveling to every country on the face of the earth (beginning most likely at Israel) and preaching the gospel with staggering results. I believe these 144,000 have been given the supernatural Bible gift of languages (tongues) and can speak in all the languages on the earth. My projection is that approximately ¼ of the earth's remaining population after the rapture are saved (born again) in short order! The other ¾ of the population fall into one of two camps. My projection is that approximately ½ of the earth's population immediately believe the Devil's lie totally or at least accept it as plausible. The final ¼ of the population are skeptics, but still not believers. It is my belief that the bulk of these ¼ who are skeptics will eventually get saved during the tribulation period as events continue to unfold. A very few in the plausible crowd may eventually be won over, but not the bulk of them.

Back-up verses for Mass Revival:

Matthew 24:14 – "¹⁴ And **this gospel of the kingdom shall be preached in all the world for a witness unto all nations**; and then shall the end come."

Mark 13:10 – "¹⁰ And **the gospel must first be published among all nations**."

Revelation 7:9-14 – "⁹ After this I beheld, and, lo, **a great multitude, which no man could number, of all nations, and kindreds, and people, and tongues, stood before the throne, and before the Lamb, clothed with white robes**, and palms in their hands; [10] and cried with a loud voice, saying, Salvation to our God which sitteth upon the throne, and unto the Lamb. [11] And all the angels stood round about the throne, and *about* the elders and the four beasts, and fell before the throne on their faces, and worshipped God, [12] saying, Amen: Blessing, and glory, and wisdom, and thanksgiving, and honour, and power, and might, *be* unto our God for ever and ever. Amen. [13] And one of the elders answered, saying unto me, What are these which are arrayed in white robes? and whence came they? [14] And I said unto him, Sir, thou knowest. And he said to me, **These are they which came out of great tribulation, and have washed their robes, and made them white in the blood of the Lamb."**

It is interesting that this mass revival is mentioned in the context of the Seven Year Tribulation Period and in Revelation chapter 7 it is specifically associated with the 144,000 Jewish witnesses, leading us to believe that these witnesses are the catalyst for the worldwide revival that takes place early in the tribulation period. It is my belief that the rapture prepares these people to receive the LORD Jesus Christ as their Saviour and become the early tribulation saints. I believe both Revelation 6:9-11 and Revelation 7:9-14 refer to the same group of redeemed & murdered early tribulation saints!

<u>Front 2 – Mass Murder:</u> After the rapture, the Devil immediately influences a world leader to sign a peace treaty with the nation of Israel (most likely many other nations are also included in this peace treaty). Then this leader yokes up with the most powerful nation on the face of the earth (Mystery Babylon the Great – the United States of America) and convinces the bulk of the US population, the UN, and much of the world's population that all followers of Jesus Christ must be

immediately murdered to prevent another event like the vanishing of millions from ever happening again. I believe the Devil will propagate a lie to explain the rapture. My guess is that the lie is or was something like this:

The followers of Jesus Christ (born again Bible believers) conspired with an extra-terrestrial alien species to snatch all infants and young children from the face of the earth. Therefore anyone across the globe who professes faith in Jesus Christ must be immediately turned in to the authorities and executed to prevent such an event from ever happening again. This will all happen in the name of peace and security.

Back-up verses for Mass Murder of early tribulation saints:

Matthew 24:9-13 – "⁹ Then shall they deliver you up to be afflicted, **and shall kill you: and ye shall be hated of all nations for my name's sake**. ¹⁰ And then shall many be offended, and shall betray one another, and shall hate one another. ¹¹ And many false prophets shall rise, and shall deceive many. ¹² And because iniquity shall abound, the love of many shall wax cold. ¹³ But he that shall endure unto the end, the same shall be saved."

Mark 13:9-13 – "⁹ But take heed to yourselves: for they shall deliver you up to councils; and in the synagogues ye shall be beaten: **and ye shall be brought before rulers and kings for my sake, for a testimony against them**. ¹⁰ And the gospel must first be published among all nations. ¹¹ But when they shall lead *you*, and deliver you up, take no thought beforehand what ye shall speak, neither do ye premeditate: but whatsoever shall be given you in that hour, that speak ye: for it is not ye that speak, but the Holy Ghost. [12] **Now the brother shall betray the brother to death, and the father the son; and children shall rise up against** *their* **parents, and shall cause them to be put to death**. [13] And ye shall be hated of all *men* for my name's sake: but he that shall endure unto the end, the same shall be saved.

Revelation 6:7-11 – "[7] And when he had opened the fourth seal, I heard the voice of the fourth beast say, Come and see. [8] And I looked, and behold a pale horse: and **his name that sat on him was Death, and Hell followed with him. And power was given unto them over the fourth part of the earth, to kill with sword, and with hunger, and with death, and with the beasts of the earth.**

[9] And when he had opened the fifth seal, **I saw under the altar the souls of them that were slain for the word of God, and for the testimony which they held:** [10] **and they cried with a loud voice, saying, How long, O Lord, holy and true, dost thou not judge and avenge our blood on them that dwell on the earth?** [11] **And white robes were given unto every one of them; and it was said unto them, that they should rest yet for a little season, until their fellowservants also and their brethren, that should be killed as they** *were,* **should be fulfilled.**"

Revelation 17:4-6 – "[4] And the woman was arrayed in purple and scarlet colour, and decked with gold and precious stones and pearls, having a golden cup in her hand full of abominations and filthiness of her fornication: [5] and upon her forehead *was* a name written, **MYSTERY, BABYLON THE GREAT, THE MOTHER OF HARLOTS AND ABOMINATIONS OF THE EARTH.** [6] And I saw the woman drunken with the blood of the saints, and with the blood of the martyrs of Jesus: and when I saw her, I wondered with great admiration.”

Revelation 18:20 – “[20] Rejoice over her, *thou* heaven, and *ye* holy apostles and prophets; for God hath avenged you on her.”

WOW! This idea of the mass murder of the early tribulation saints is scriptural!

Now I do believe that the context of 2nd Thessalonians 2:9-12 is in reference to a different lie from the Devil - the false resurrection of the Beast (the Antichrist) at the halfway point of the Seven Year Tribulation Period. Those who rejected the truth of the preaching of God's two special witnesses at Jerusalem and the 144,000 Jewish witnesses during the first three and half year of the tribulation period, are those who will believe the lie of Satan and accept the false resurrection of the Antichrist, taking the Mark of the Beast. They will be sent strong delusion by God Himself, because they rejected the truth as preached by the two special witnesses and the 144,000 Jewish witnesses.

2nd Thessalonians 2:9-12 – “[9] *Even him,* whose coming is after the working of Satan with all power and signs and lying wonders, [10] and with all deceivableness of unrighteousness in them that perish; because they received not the love of the truth, that they might be saved. [11] **And for this cause God shall send them strong delusion, that they should believe a lie:** [12] **that they all might be damned who believed not the truth, but had pleasure in unrighteousness.”**

That being said, I also believe that those who had the most gospel influence before the rapture, but did not get saved (primarily the citizens of the United States of America) will be among the most likely to believe and propagate the Devil's lie to explain the vanishings after the rapture. Early in the tribulation period it is my belief that Satan himself will influence the United States of America (Mystery Babylon the Great) to lead all the other nations of the world to report all newly saved tribulation saints to the authorities where they will be murdered in mass to supposedly prevent another disappearance!

I believe one quarter of the earth's population will be killed fairly early in the tribulation period (Revelation 6:7-11); the bulk of these being the newly redeemed tribulation saints. Their own family members will turn them in because they believe the Devil's lie and fear another future event like the rapture! Read the verses above again and interpret them literally. These means that ¼ of the earth's population (mainly new tribulation saints) are killed early in the first half of the tribulation period. One quarter of the earth's population based on my numbers (page 6) equals **1,793,020,780 people.** That is **1 Billion, 793 Million, 20 thousand, seven hundred, and eighty people** – all murdered for putting their faith in the LORD Jesus Christ early in the tribulation period (Daniel's 70th Week) shortly after the rapture!

I am not sure if these events of **Mass Revival & Mass Murder** have already happened at the time you are reading this, but either way I beg you to please get born again immediately and line up on the side of Jesus Christ and His people – this includes born again tribulation saints and the Nation of Israel!

Chapter 4: The Role of the United States of America During the Seven Year Tribulation Period

Real Time Update: 1003 Hours; May 04, 2017: The rapture (catching up) of all truly born again believers (redeemed saints) has not happened yet at the time of this writing – although I expect it very soon. United States President Donald Trump just met with the Palestinian President Mahmoud Abbas. See the excerpt below with a link at the bottom and then see the excerpt response by the Israelis Prime Minister Benjamin Netanyahu with another link at the bottom:

"READ IN FULL: Trump and Abbas' Remarks After First Meeting in White House

The full statements made by President Donald Trump and Palestinian President Mahmoud Abbas

Haaretz, May 03, 2017 9:07 PM

REMARKS BY PRESIDENT TRUMP AND PRESIDENT ABBAS OF THE PALESTINIAN AUTHORITY IN JOINT STATEMENT

PRESIDENT TRUMP: Thank you very much. Today I am pleased to welcome President Abbas to the White House for his first to Washington in quite a while. Almost 24 years ago, it was on these grounds that President Abbas stood with a courageous peacemaker, then-Israeli Prime Minister Yitzhak Rabin. Here at the White House, President Abbas signed a Declaration of Principles -- very important -- which laid the foundation for peace between the Israelis and Palestinians.

The President -- Mr. President, you signed your name to the first Israeli-Palestinian peace agreement. You remember that well, right? And I want to support you in being the Palestinian leader who signs his name to the final and most important peace agreement that brings safety, stability, and prosperity to both peoples and to the region…"

http://www.haaretz.com/us-news/1.787109

"In First Reaction to Trump Meet, Netanyahu Says Abbas Lied, but Hopes Peace Is Possible

Palestinian 'name their schools after mass murderers of Israelis and they pay terrorists,' Netanyahu says.

Barak Ravid, May 04, 2017, 1:43 PM

Prime Minister Benjamin Netanyahu gave his first reaction to the meeting between U.S. President Trump and Palestinian President Abbas during his meeting with the Romanian prime minister on Thursday in Jerusalem, saying "I look forward to discussing with President Trump the best ways to advance peace. This is something we fervently share with the president. "I heard President Abbas yesterday say that the Palestinians teach their children peace. Unfortunately, that's not true. They name their schools after mass murderers of Israelis and they pay terrorists. But I hope that it's possible to achieve a change and to pursue a genuine peace. This is something Israel is always ready for. I'm always ready for genuine peace."

http://www.haaretz.com/israel-news/1.787286

Enough with real time updates and back to the book. In this chapter I want to go through a number of scriptures and discuss the role of the United States of America during the Seven Year Tribulation Period on the earth. If it is already clear to the (post rapture) tribulation saints that the United States of America is the superpower nation "MYSTERY BABYLON THE GREAT, THE MOTHER OF HARLOTS AND ABOMINATIONS OF THE EARTH", then you can edit or delete much of this chapter and only provide the information necessary for the tribulation saints. Much of the scriptures and information provided are intended for my fellow American church age believers who may happen to read this book before the rapture. Most of them view the scriptures through patriotic American colored glasses and seem to have a hard time accepting the literal interpretation of certain scriptures with regards to this end time nation – MYSTERY BABYLON THE GREAT.

<u>Qualifier 1 – The LORD is in control:</u> **For those of you reading this before the rapture, before I go any further, I want to lay out a few qualifiers. I am fully aware that the LORD can easily pull down one nation and raise up another. For example, if He chooses to rapture the church age saints 100 years from now and not in the near future, He could bring to nothing the United States of America and easily raise up another nation that matches the prophetic scriptures perfectly. He is God and can do whatsoever He pleases! God could also bring a mass revival to the United States of America, where a large percentage of her population get born again. Then after the rapture of believers, another nation could take over the land mass and the economic engine of the United States of America due to her depleted population. This new nation could quickly and easily become Mystery Babylon the Great.**

All that being said, I do believe with all my heart that if the LORD chooses to rapture His church age saints in the next couple of decades (with no mass revival in America) and if the United States continues as a superpower nation (the hammer of the whole earth) during this time, then she is definitely that nation that fulfills the prophecies of Mystery Babylon the Great. Mystery Babylon the Great is completely destroyed at the very end of the Seven Year Tribulation Period on the earth and never will be inhabited again after her destruction. My fellow pre-rapture church age believers in America need to realize that this destruction happens after the rapture near the very end of the Seven Year Tribulation Period.

Qualifier 2 – Some prophecies have both a partial fulfillment in past history and a full/complete/literal fulfillment in the future: An example of this is the prophecies around the virgin birth of our Messiah in Isaiah 7:10-16 with the literal complete future fulfillment of Isaiah 7:14 occurring in Matthew 1:22-23 when our Messiah, the LORD Jesus Christ (God in the flesh), was miraculously born to the virgin Mary. To deny this principle in relation to the second coming of Jesus and end time future events, means you must also deny this principle in relation to the first coming of the LORD Jesus Christ! Bottom line: a partial fulfillment of a prophecy in history does not negate the future complete literal fulfillment of the same prophecy. God will always keep His word completely and the scripture cannot be broken! It is totally obvious that a multitude of prophecies concerning nations have not yet been fulfilled and have a full literally fulfillment yet in the future. The scriptures truly record 100% accurate history before it is written, and have never missed and will never miss on one iota of future prophecy!

<u>Qualifier 3 – I will do my best to avoid two extremes in my examination of the United States of America:</u> In all of my research for this book I found two extremes in present day 2017, concerning end times prophesy and the United States of America. First there is a group of people made up of both believers and unbelievers that definitely believe America is Mystery Babylon the Great. Most believers in this group think incorrectly that they will have to go through all or part of the tribulation period. Also most in this group (believers and unbelievers alike) see little to no redeeming qualities in America's founding and past history. They are quick to point out conspiracy theories related to groups such as the Council of Foreign Relations (CFR), the Illuminati, the Masons, the International Monetary Fund & the World Bank, etc. Even though there may be a lot of nuggets of truth in what many of these teachers are saying, I believe it is much like someone who cannot see the forest for the trees. There has always been an evil attack on the United States of America, but I contend that this attack and many of these afore mentioned groups are orchestrated & directed by none other than the Devil himself (Ephesians 6:10-12). I also believe that America definitely did have a big Christian influence in her founding and true history points to her being founded as a Christian nation. Just because Satan has attacked her that does not mean that God has failed to use her for much good around the world through her elevation of the LORD Jesus Christ and Christianity.

The other extreme are those people (generally born again faithful Christians) who see everything about America through patriotic rose colored glasses. They sometimes worship the idol of American patriotism more than the LORD Jesus Christ Himself. You speak the truth about modern day wickedness in America and her negative influence around the world, then you are lumped with the first group that sees the Devil behind every bush in the good ole USA. In the eyes of this patriotic group, if you even think about speaking against American patriotism, you might as well have spoken anathema against the LORD Jesus Christ Himself! Most in this group see America as the country that rid the world of Nazism in World War II, and fail to see that the average citizen of America today is biblically illiterate and has simply a form of godliness without any power. This form of Christianity is generally (there are exceptions) a far cry from the Christianity of the average citizen of this country in the past, during one of her great awakenings and periods of revival. Even the popular mantra today is: "Make America Great Again", and this is hardly ever talking about her Christian influence, but her economic and military might!

In this analysis I want to simply look at the Bible and see what the scriptures say about the end time nation of Mystery Babylon the Great. If the shoe fits the United States of America today, especially after the rapture when her Christian influence is totally gone, then we in the USA need to wear that shoe and own it – no matter how much it hurts! Jeremiah was condemned for preaching that Israel would go into Babylonian captivity, but he still preached the truth of God's prophetic word in spite of those in Israel who fought against him!

The Law of Probability as Related to Prophecy

I have rarely heard this discussed in relation to end time events concerning certain countries or nations. But common sense would tell you that as you get more prophecies that fit a certain nation, the likelihood of that nation being the fulfillment of the prophecies greatly increases. For illustration purposes let me explain:

Let us assume we have a pro football stadium of 50,000 fans and you are trying to identify a certain fan in that stadium by giving a description without saying the fan's name directly (the name is a **mystery**). First you say the fan is a man – that leaves us around 25,000 fans. Then you say he is 51 years old. That leaves us around 400 fans. Then you say he is 5'-8" tall. That leaves around 30 fans. Then you say he is bald. That leaves us around 8 fans. Finally you say he weighs exactly 185 pounds, and only one fan from the 50,000 fits that exact description. We went from **50,000** fans to just **1**, by simply listing five characteristics that were fulfilled in that one fan: 1) he is a man; 2) he is 51 years old; 3) he is 5'-8" tall; 4) he is bald; and 5) he weighs exactly 185 pounds. A lot of people in the stadium may fit any single one of those characteristics, but only one person fits all five of these characteristics.

Now let us think about this with regards to nations or countries, and which nation fits the Bible description of Mystery Babylon the Great. The very fact that the LORD uses the term "**MYSTERY** BABYLON THE GREAT..." in the book of Revelation gives us a strong indication that the exact name of this nation is meant to be a mystery until the end times when the prophecy is close to fulfilment. Before this time there may not even be a single nation that fits this description completely, but as we move closer to the rapture and tribulation period the picture becomes clearer to students of Bible prophecy. The word **"MYSTERY"** is also a strong indication that this nation is NOT the nation of Babylon itself, but a nation with similar characteristics to that of ancient Babylon.

Additionally, the number of nations on the planet is not 50,000, but only 195 as of 2017. Therefore the pool of nations that possibly could by Mystery Babylon the Great is not that big. Furthermore we must realize that some prophecies concerning this nation may not be fulfilled until the Seven Year Tribulation Period itself. So whether you are reading this before the rapture or after the rapture makes a difference with regards to the fulfillment of these prophecies. Let us look at a few things in the Bible that relate to this nation that is destroyed for her sins at the end of the Seven Year Tribulation Period.

Now I want to go through the books of Jeremiah chapters 50 and 51, Revelation chapters 17 and 18, and other portions of scripture to look at the characteristics of this end time superpower nation – **MYSTERY BABYLON THE GREAT.** For the sake of this discussion we will call this nation "She", but I believe this nation is none other than the **United States of America**.

The Bible Characteristics of Mystery Babylon the Great

1) She has a large Jewish population and it appears as if most of them escape before her utter destruction. Her destruction causes the Jews to turn their hearts to Jerusalem and seek the LORD their God.

Jeremiah 50:4-8 – "⁴ In those days, and in that time, saith the Lord, the children of Israel shall come, they and the children of Judah together, going and

weeping: **they shall go, and seek the Lord their God.** [5] They shall ask the way to Zion with their faces thitherward, saying, Come, and let us join ourselves to the Lord in a perpetual covenant that shall not be forgotten."

[6] My people hath been lost sheep: their shepherds have caused them to go astray, they have turned them away on the mountains: they have gone from mountain to hill, they have forgotten their restingplace. [7]All that found them have devoured them: and their adversaries said, We offend not, because they have sinned against the Lord, the habitation of justice, even the Lord, the hope of their fathers. [8] **Remove out of the midst of Babylon**, and go forth out of the land of the Chaldeans, and be as the he goats before the flocks."

Jeremiah 51:5-6 – "[5] For Israel *hath* not *been* forsaken, nor Judah of his God, of the Lord of hosts; though their land was filled with sin against the Holy One of Israel. [6] **Flee out of the midst of Babylon, and deliver every man his soul: be not cut off in her iniquity**; for this *is* the time of the Lord's vengeance; he will render unto her a recompence."

Isaiah 48:20 – "[20] Go ye forth of Babylon, flee ye from the Chaldeans, with a voice of singing declare ye, tell this, utter it *even* to the end of the earth; say ye, **The Lord hath redeemed his servant Jacob.**"

Zechariah 2:6-9 – "[6] Ho, ho, *come forth*, and flee from the land of the north, saith the Lord: for I have spread you abroad as the four winds of the heaven, saith the Lord. [7] **Deliver thyself, O Zion, that dwellest *with* the**

daughter of Babylon. [8] For thus saith the Lord of hosts; After the glory hath he sent me unto the nations which spoiled you: for he that toucheth you toucheth the apple of his eye. [9] For, behold, I will shake mine hand upon them, and they shall be a spoil to their servants: and ye shall know that the Lord of hosts hath sent me."

Let us look at the top 10 countries around the world with regards to their Core Jewish population as of 2013. The total Core Jewish population at this time is estimated to be approximately 14 million 200 thousand people. These numbers that follow only include the Core Jewish Population as the Enlarged Jewish population is greater and estimated to be closer to 20 Million people.

	Country	Core Jewish population	% of total
1	Israel	6,014,300	43.4%
2	United States	5,425,000	39.2%
3	France	478,000	3.5%
4	Canada	380,000	2.7%
5	United Kingdom	290,000	2.1%
6	Russian Federation	190,000	1.4%
7	Argentina	181,500	1.3%
8	Germany	118,000	0.9%
9	Australia	112,500	0.8%
10	Brazil	95,200	0.7%

Source: the Jewish Data Bank (Table 4), the 10 countries as of 2013 with the largest core Jewish populations

As you can see there is no other country with a greater percentage of the Jewish population than the United States of America other than the nation of Israel itself. Some sources place the Jewish population of the United States at greater than 7 million people and even greater than the nation of Israel. The United States has at least around 40% of the world's Core Jewish population. How can Jews flee from a country where they do not reside?

It is my belief that this last great exodus of the Jewish people from the United States of America near the end of the tribulation period, along with the follow on 1-hour nuclear destruction of the United States of America, removes the last idol for these Jewish hold outs that have still NOT turned their hearts toward Jesus as their true Messiah during the tribulation period! A few Jewish holdouts truly trust the United States of America for their deliverance right up to her end. The coming of the LORD Jesus Christ in power in glory at the battle of Armageddon (Revelation chapter 19) follows shortly after the utter destruction of the United States of America (Revelation chapters 17 and 18).

As is always the case, the LORD blesses all other nations through Israel and I believe many of the tribulation saints who are still hiding and living in the United States of America also escape out of the country just before her utter destruction. The LORD warns his people to escape according to the scriptures and even uses rumors and an angel to pronounce judgment on Mystery Babylon before her utter destruction. See the verses that follow:

Jeremiah 51:41-47 – "⁴¹ How is Sheshach taken! and how is the praise of the whole earth surprised! **how is**

Babylon become an astonishment among the nations!
[42] The sea is come up upon Babylon: she is covered with the multitude of the waves thereof. [43] **Her cities are a desolation**, a dry land, and a wilderness, a land wherein no man dwelleth, neither doth *any* son of man pass thereby.

[44] And I will punish Bel in Babylon, and I will bring forth out of his mouth that which he hath swallowed up: **and the nations shall not flow together any more unto him: yea, the wall of Babylon shall fall.** [45] **My people, go ye out of the midst of her, and deliver ye every man his soul from the fierce anger of the Lord.** [46] And lest your heart faint, and ye fear for the rumour that shall be heard in the land; **a rumour shall both come *one* year, and after that in *another* year *shall come* a rumour, and violence in the land, ruler against ruler.** [47] Therefore, behold, the days come, that I will do judgment upon the graven images of Babylon: and her whole land shall be confounded, and all her slain shall fall in the midst of her."

Revelation 14:8 – "[8] And there followed another angel, saying, **Babylon is fallen, is fallen, that great city, because she made all nations drink of the wine of the wrath of her fornication.**"

Revelation 18:1-2 – "[1] And after these things I saw another angel come down from heaven, having great power; and the earth was lightened with his glory. [2] And he cried mightily with a strong voice, saying, **Babylon the great is fallen, is fallen, and is become the habitation of devils**, and the hold of every foul spirit, and a cage of every unclean and hateful bird.

2) She is a very young nation with a mother nation.

Jeremiah 50:12 - "¹² Your **mother** shall be sore confounded; she that bare you shall be ashamed: behold, **the hindermost of the nations** shall be a wilderness, a dry land, and a desert."

This is very interesting as the United States of America among major nations is very young. Other nations such as Greece, Spain, Italy, Egypt, Syria, Ethiopia, etc., we read about their existence in the Bible. These nations are thousands of years old. We (the United States of America) just became a country a little over 230 years ago in 1783. Furthermore we have just been recognized as a superpower over the last 100 years and mainly after the defeat of Nazi Germany in World War II. America is very young in the grand scheme of things. With regards to major nations on the earth, we truly are **the hindermost of nations!**

Also **the United States of America definitely has a mother nation** – none other than **Great Britain!** The British Colonies became the American Colonies after the Continental Army (army of the colonies), led by none other than George Washington, defeated the British Empire Army in what historians call the American Revolutionary War (1775 to 1783). In 1783 the Treaty of Paris was signed by the British King, George III, recognizing the newly created independent nation as the United States of America.

This one verse (Jeremiah 50:12) limits itself to which nation could be the future Babylon that will be completely destroyed by fire and left totally desolate and uninhabited near the end of the Seven Year Tribulation Period. But let us continue.

3) **She is a nation of immigrants.**

Jeremiah 50:37 – "³⁷ A sword is upon their horses, and upon their chariots, and upon **all the mingled people that are in the midst of her**; and they shall become as women: a sword is upon her treasures; and they shall be robbed."

Jeremiah 51:44 – "⁴⁴ And I will punish Bel in Babylon, and I will bring forth out of his mouth that which he hath swallowed up: **and the nations shall not flow together any more unto him**: yea, the wall of Babylon shall fall."

Revelation 17:15 – "¹⁵ And he saith unto me, **The waters** which thou sawest, where the whore sitteth, **are peoples, and multitudes, and nations, and tongues**."

This is really interesting as there is probably not one nation on the face of the earth besides the United States of America that is made up almost entirely of immigrants. Only a very small percentage of the citizens of the United States are Native American Indians – that is why she is called the melting pot nation. That brings us to the next characteristic of this nation.

4) **She appears to have a large percentage of people that claim other nations as their home.**

The verses that follow encourage her inhabitants to flee to their own countries before her destruction. What is interesting about this is that the percentage of unassimilated people living in America seems to have greatly increased over the last 40 years. A policy of open borders, unenforced immigration law, and a general tolerance toward illegal immigration (whether right or wrong) has led to this situation.

Jeremiah 50:16 – "[16] Cut off the sower from Babylon, and him that handleth the sickle in the time of harvest: **for fear of the oppressing sword they shall turn every one to his people, and they shall flee every one to his own land.**"

Jeremiah 51:9 – "[9] We would have healed Babylon, but she is not healed: **forsake her, and let us go every one into his own country**: for her judgment reacheth unto heaven, and is lifted up *even* to the skies.

Isaiah 13:14 – "And it shall be as the chased roe, and as a sheep that no man taketh up: **they shall every man turn to his own people, and flee every one into his own land.**"

5) She is a military superpower nation.

Jeremiah 50:23 – "[23] How is **the hammer of the whole earth** cut asunder and broken! how is Babylon become a desolation among the nations!"

Jeremiah 51:53 – "[53] Though Babylon **should mount up to heaven, and though she should fortify the height of her strength**, *yet* from me shall spoilers come unto her, saith the Lord."

These two verses describe both the offensive and defensive military power of Mystery Babylon the Great. She is the hammer of the whole earth which describes her as the world's policeman and an offensive military power. What other nation in modern times can be called the hammer of the whole earth, but the United States of America? The only one that may even come close is Russia. The U.S. has a presence in many other countries with her military power. According to the 2015 Base Structure Report published by the Department of Defense the United States has 513 overseas military sites (see the link below). All other countries pale in comparison to the U.S. and many if not most countries have no overseas military presence.

http://www.acq.osd.mil/eie/Downloads/BSI/Base%20Structure%20Report%20FY15.pdf

Jeremiah 51:53 seems to clearly indicate that Mystery Babylon has military capability that reaches even to space. The U.S. military has for many years been using satellite technology to gather intelligence and defend against potential attacks. The move to accelerate her space defenses is ongoing and I believe she has even more capability than that which is published. See the following link to the 2016 article on this subject by CNN:

http://www.cnn.com/2016/11/28/politics/space-war-us-military-preparations/

This report matches perfectly with Jeremiah 51:53 as the defenses of the United States of America which up to the first and second heaven (the sky and space). How many other countries have this kind of military defense?

6) She is a very rich nation and a consumer of the world's goods.

Jeremiah 51:13 – "¹³ O thou that dwellest upon many waters, **abundant in treasures**, thine end is come, *and* the measure of thy covetousness."

Revelation 18:11-19 – "¹¹ **And the merchants of the earth shall weep and mourn over her; for no man buyeth their merchandise any more**: ¹² the merchandise of gold, and silver, and precious stones, and of pearls, and fine linen, and purple, and silk, and scarlet, and all thyine wood, and all manner vessels of ivory, and all manner vessels of most precious wood, and of brass, and iron, and marble, ¹³ and cinnamon, and odours, and ointments, and frankincense, and wine, and oil, and fine flour, and wheat, and beasts, and sheep, and horses, and chariots, and slaves, and souls of men. ¹⁴ **And the fruits that thy soul lusted after are departed from thee, and all things which were dainty and goodly are departed from thee, and thou shalt find them no more at all.** ¹⁵ The merchants of these things, **which were made rich by her**, shall stand afar off for the fear of her torment, weeping and wailing, ¹⁶ and saying, Alas, alas, that great city, that was clothed in fine linen, and purple, and scarlet, and **decked with gold, and precious stones, and pearls! ¹⁷ For in one hour so great riches is come to nought.** And every shipmaster, and all the company in ships, and sailors, and as many as trade by sea, stood afar off, ¹⁸ and cried when they saw the smoke of her burning, saying, What *city is* like unto this great city! ¹⁹ And they cast dust on their heads, and cried, weeping and wailing, saying, **Alas, alas, that great city, wherein were made**

rich all that had ships in the sea by reason of her costliness! for in one hour is she made desolate."

This fact does not need an explanation. Almost everybody in the world knows that the poorest people living in America, are rich in comparison to the rest of the globe's population. See the 2015 article that follows where America is listed as the number one consumer of the world's goods with 29% of these goods consumed in America.

http://www.internationalbusinessguide.org/25-largest-consumers-markets-outlook-2015/

What is very interesting about this statistic is that two facts are ignored. First, many of the countries in the top 25 among consumers get a substantial amount of their income through American tourism and American immigration (immigrants in America sending money back to relatives in their home country). Second, according to the Census Bureau, the USA only makes up 4.4 of the world's population, with 319.4 million people in the USA and 7.2 billion people in the entire world. That means that the average American consumes approximately 9 times the amount of goods as the average person across the rest of the globe. The United States of America is truly by far the richest nation on the face of the earth and the number one consumer of the world's goods.

7) She is a very proud nation given to idolatry.

Isaiah 47:5-9 – "⁵ Sit thou silent, and get thee into darkness, O daughter of the Chaldeans: for thou shalt no more be called, The lady of kingdoms. ⁶ I was wroth with my people, I have polluted mine inheritance, and given them into thine hand: thou didst shew them no mercy; upon the ancient hast thou very heavily laid thy yoke. ⁷ And thou saidst, I shall be a lady for ever: *so* that thou didst not lay these *things* to thy heart, neither didst remember the latter end of it. ⁸ **Therefore hear now this, *thou that art* given to pleasures, that dwellest carelessly, that sayest in thine heart, I *am*, and none else beside me; I shall not sit *as* a widow, neither shall I know the loss of children**: ⁹ but these two *things* shall come to thee in a moment in one day, the loss of children, and widowhood: they shall come upon thee in their perfection for the multitude of thy sorceries, *and* for the great abundance of thine enchantments."

Jeremiah 50:29-32 – "²⁹ Call together the archers against Babylon: all ye that bend the bow, camp against it round about; let none thereof escape: recompense her according to her work; according to all that she hath done, do unto her: **for she hath been proud against the Lord, against the Holy One of Israel**.

³⁰ Therefore shall her young men fall in the streets, and all her men of war shall be cut off in that day, saith the Lord. ³¹ Behold, **I *am* against thee, *O thou* most proud**, saith the Lord God of hosts: for thy day is come, the time *that* I will visit thee. ³² **And the most proud shall stumble and fall, and none shall raise him up**: and I will kindle a fire in his cities, and it shall devour all round about him."

Jeremiah 50:2 – "² Declare ye among the nations, and publish, and set up a standard; publish, *and* conceal not: say, Babylon is taken, Bel is confounded, Merodach is broken in pieces; **her idols are confounded, her images are broken in pieces.**"

Jeremiah 50:38 – "³⁸ A drought *is* upon her waters; and they shall be dried up: **for it *is* the land of graven images, and they are mad upon *their* idols.**"

8) **She appears to be a nation made rich because of the LORD's past blessings, but a nation that has since turned toward wickedness and polluted the other nations of the world.**

Jeremiah 51:7 – "⁷ Babylon *hath been* a golden cup in the LORD'S hand, that made all the earth drunken: the nations have drunken of her wine; therefore the nations are mad."

Revelation 17:1-2 – "¹**And there came one of the seven angels which had the seven vials, and talked with me, saying unto me, Come hither;** I will shew unto thee the judgment of the great whore that sitteth upon many waters: ² with whom the kings of the earth have committed fornication, and the inhabitants of the earth have been made drunk with the wine of her fornication.**"

Recently I attended camp with the teenagers of our church. This camp happened to be the week of the fourth of July and the preacher (a very good preacher, whom I highly respect) was preaching on July 4ᵗʰ about how the LORD has blessed America. I almost fell out of my chair as he was preaching and he said just about the exact words of Jeremiah 51:7. He said: **"America has been a golden cup in God's hand!"** He went on to say how the LORD truly had blessed the United States of America in its founding. I seriously do not think this preacher even knew that he was quoting Jeremiah 51:7a - wow!

I could easily list five or six more characteristics of Mystery Babylon the Great that fit the modern day United States of America. But the purpose of this book is to help the tribulation saints and NOT to convince pre-rapture church age saints that the United States of America is very likely Mystery Babylon the Great of the Bible.

<u>Chapter 5</u>: The 70 Weeks of Daniel and How Do I Count Days during the Seven Year Tribulation Period?

Real Time Update: 1400 Hours; November 5, 2018: It has been two years since I started this book and things on the politically scene are coming true as I projected two years ago before Donald Trump became President of the United States. Based on the last chapter you know that I truly believe that America is Mystery Babylon the Great as foretold in the Bible. For America to be a superpower nation after the rapture she has to have economic and military growth before the rapture in my opinion, because the rapture will involve the disappearance of many Christians (see page 6 of this book for my estimation on the number of people raptured in the United States of America). This is why over two years ago I went against the polls and projected that Donald Trump would surprisingly win the Presidency of the United States, which he did. His campaign slogan was and is: "Make America Great Again!" Is this a coincidence that the end-times superpower nation during the tribulation period is titled Mystery Babylon the Great? I do not think so! As I expected after his election in 2016, America's economy is now booming, her military is expanding and growing, she is making better trade deals that make her even richer, and the typical Christian in the United States is sitting on their blessed assurance with little to no expectation of the rapture.

This is surely a time in history as it was in the days of Noah and Lot, with very few people, including most Christians, expecting or looking for the rapture and the follow on Seven Year Tribulation Period. It is surely at a time in history as predicted in the scriptures when people least expect these events. Under

President Obama almost all Pre-Tribulation Prophecy teachers were looking for the rapture, based on the premise that America would fall and crumble before the Seven Year Tribulation Period, because she is not mentioned in prophecy. The problem with this line of thinking is that their premise was totally wrong – America is mentioned in prophecy. America will not crumble after the rapture, but she will be the fulfillment of the end-times superpower nation: **Mystery Babylon the Great!** *She will be very great again, just not great for God, but great for the Antichrist! The Antichrist will use her power and might during the Seven Year Tribulation Period, then he will destroy her at the very end of the tribulation period (See Revelation chapters 17 & 18 and Jeremiah chapters 50 & 51).*

Now I want to transition into the 70 weeks of Daniel and I want to show how we know that the Tribulation Period will be a Seven Year period, consisting of 84 months, or 2520 days (based on a 30 day per month prophetic calendar). See the study that follows and please do the math.

A Study of the 70 Weeks of Daniel

References:
> - The King James Bible: Daniel 9:20-27
> - *The Coming Prince* by Sir Robert Anderson – first published in 1894. (https://www.whatsaiththescripture.com/Text.Only/pdfs/ The_Coming_Prince_Text.pdf)
> - *Daniel: Verse by verse study* by Oliver B. Greene – published in 1964 (http://www.geocities.ws/kjvbiblestudytools3/0080.pdf)

Daniel 9:20-27 – "**20** And whiles I *was* speaking, and praying, and confessing my sin and the sin of my people Israel, and presenting my supplication before the Lord my God for the holy mountain of my God; **21** yea, whiles I *was* speaking in prayer, **even the man Gabriel, whom I had seen in the vision at the beginning, being caused to fly swiftly, touched me** about the time of the evening oblation. **22** And he informed *me*, and talked with me, and said, **O Daniel, I am now come forth to give thee skill and understanding**. **23** At the beginning of thy supplications the commandment came forth, and I am come to shew *thee;* for thou *art* greatly beloved: therefore understand the matter, and consider the vision. **24** Seventy weeks are determined upon thy people and upon thy holy city, to finish the transgression, and to make an end of sins, and to make reconciliation for iniquity, and to bring in everlasting righteousness, and to seal up the vision and prophecy, and to anoint the most Holy. **25** Know therefore and understand, *that* from the going forth of the commandment to restore and to build Jerusalem unto the Messiah the Prince *shall be* seven weeks, and threescore and two weeks: the street shall be built again, and the wall, even in troublous times. **26** And after threescore and two weeks shall Messiah be cut off, but not for himself: and the people of the prince that shall come shall destroy the city and the sanctuary; and the end thereof *shall be* with a flood, and unto the end of the war desolations are determined. **27** And he shall confirm the covenant with many for one week: and in the midst of the week he shall cause the sacrifice and the oblation to cease, and for the overspreading of abominations he shall make *it* desolate, even until the consummation, and that determined shall be poured upon the desolate."**

Question: How long is a prophetic week or Daniel's 70th week yet to be fulfilled?

> ➤ Let us look at the **69 weeks** (seven weeks and threescore and two weeks) prophecy that has already been fulfilled.

> ➤ **The Beginning of the Fulfilled Prophecy:**
>   o **The going forth of the commandment to restore and to build Jerusalem**
>   o The 1st Nisan in the twentieth year of Artaxerxes (the edict to rebuild Jerusalem) was 14th March, B.C. 445 – **See Nehemiah**

> ➤ **The End of the Fulfilled Prophecy:**
>   o **Unto the Messiah the Prince ... shall Messiah be cut off, but not for himself**
>   o Jesus was received as the Prince (the King) on His glorious entry into Jerusalem on His way to the cross to be cut off – **Zachariah 9:9; Luke 19:35-40.**
>   o The 10th Nisan in Passion Week (Christ's entry into Jerusalem) was on **6th April, A.D. 32.**

> ➤ **A Scriptural Year – This Time Period is Used in All Bible Prophecy**
>   o See **Genesis 7:11-24, 8:3-4; Revelation 11:2, 12:6, 13:5)**
>   o 5 months = 150 days, each month = 30 days. 42 months = 1260 days
>   o **Therefore a Scriptural Year = 360 days; 3 ½ Years = 1260 days**

- ➤ 14th March 445 B.C. **to 6th April 32 A.D. = 476 years and 24 days** (both days inclusive based on the language of the prophecy and one year deleted because time is kept from 1 B.C. to 1 A.D. (no zero B.C.))

- ➤ SEE THE MATH
  - o 476 years x 365 days/year = **173,740 days**
  - o 24 days =   **24 days**
  - o Leap years in this time period =   **116 days**
  - TOTAL =   173,880 days

- ➤ **69 Prophetic Weeks = 69 Weeks x 7 days/week = 483 Prophetic Days**
  - o Fulfilled prophecy = **173,880 days x 1 year/360 days = 483 years**
  - o Therefore each prophetic day in Daniel = **1 year**
  - o Therefore each prophetic week = **Seven Years**

<u>Answer:</u> **Daniel's 70th Week (one prophetic week) yet to be fulfilled = <u>Seven Years</u>**

- ❖ **This is the Seven Year Tribulation Period!**
- ❖ **It begins with the covenant of the Antichrist (the false prince) with many (many people in Israel or many nations to include Israel) for 1 prophetic week or Seven Years (Daniel 9:27; Isaiah 28:14-18).**
- ❖ **In the midst (halfway = 3 ½ years) of the week, the Antichrist breaks the covenant at the Abomination of Desolation (Daniel 9:27, Matt 24:15)**

❖ **The end of the Seven Years is at the Revelation (glorious appearing) of the LORD Jesus Christ (Revelation 19:11-21; Jude vs 14,15; Zach 14:1-4)**

CONCLUSION: This completes Book 1 of "The Tribulation Survival Manual" Series. In Book 2 of this Series we will look at the seven seal judgments. These judgments take place during the early years of the 7 year tribulation period. If these judgments have not yet occurred I would encourage to get a copy of Book 2 so you have a better understanding about the events that are about to happen on the earth.

In Christ Jesus,

Brother Paul McCarty   Galatians 6:14

Printed in Great Britain
by Amazon